DATE DUE

FEB 1 3 2014	

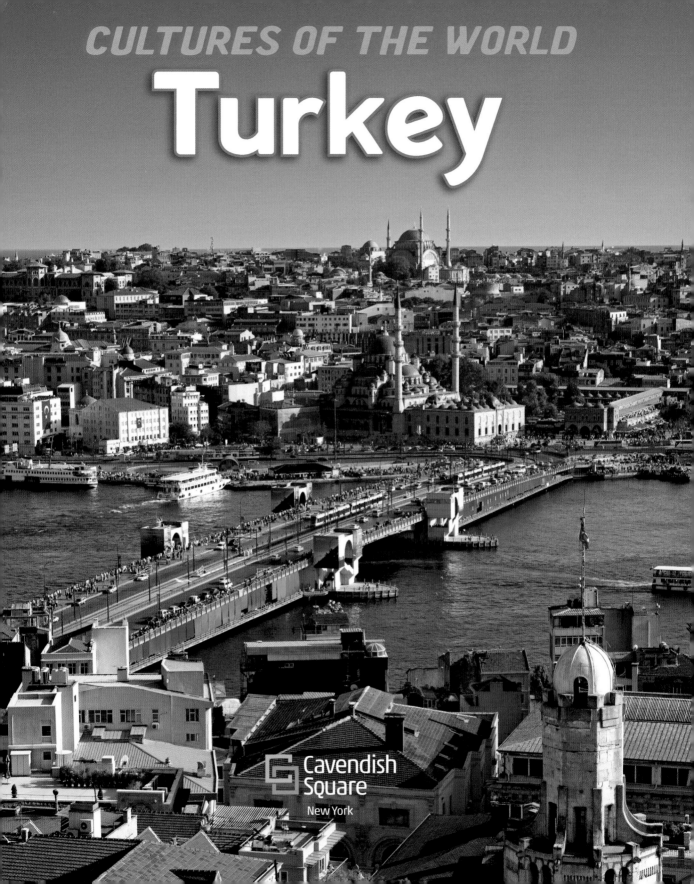

CULTURES OF THE WORLD
Turkey

Cavendish Square
New York

Published in 2014 by Cavendish Square Publishing, LLC
303 Park Avenue South, Suite 1247, New York, NY 10010

Third Edition

This publication is published with arrangement with Marshall Cavendish International (Asia) Pte Ltd.

Website: cavendishsq.com

Cultures of the World is a registered trademark of Times Publishing Limited.

This publication represents the opinions and views of the author based on his or her personal experience, knowledge, and research. The information in this book serves as a general guide only. The author and publisher have used their best efforts in preparing this book and disclaim liability rising directly or indirectly from the use and application of this book.

CPSIA Compliance Information: Batch #WW14CSQ

All websites were available and accurate when this book was sent to press.

Library of Congress Cataloging-in-Publication Data
Sheehan, Sean.
Turkey / by Sean Sheehan and Yong Jui Lin.
 p. cm. — (Cultures of the world)
Includes bibliographical references and index.
ISBN 978-0-76148-016-7 (hardcover) ISBN 978-1-62712-627-4 (paperback) ISBN 978-0-76148-024-2 (ebook)
1. Turkey — Juvenile literature. I. Sheehan, Sean, 1951-. II. Title.
DR417.4 .S54 2014
956.1—d23

Writers: Sean Sheehan and Yong Jui Lin
Editor: Mindy Pang
Designer: Lynn Chin

PICTURE CREDITS
Cover: © Eric Farrelly / Alamy
Audrius Tomonis - www.banknotes.com: 135 • Corbis / Click Photos: 24, 25, 29 • Getty Images: 101 • Inmagine.com / Alamy: 1, 3, 5, 7, 8, 10, 11, 12, 13, 14, 15, 16, 17, 18, 19, 20, 21, 22, 26, 27, 28, 30, 31, 32, 33, 34, 35, 36, 41, 42, 43, 46, 47, 48, 49, 50, 54, 59, 60, 62, 63, 64, 66, 68, 69, 70, 71, 72, 73, 74, 76, 79, 80, 81, 82, 83, 84, 86, 87, 88, 89, 90, 92, 94, 95, 96, 97, 98, 99, 100, 103, 104, 105, 106, 108, 109, 110, 112, 114, 116, 117, 118, 119, 120, 122, 123, 125, 126, 127, 128, 129, 130, 131 • Reuters: 39, 44 • Turkishculture.org: 113 • Wikimedia Commons: 85

PRECEDING PAGE
The Galata bridge and skyline of Istanbul, Turkey.

Printed in the United States of America

CONTENTS

TURKEY TODAY

TURKEY IS A EURASIAN COUNTRY LOCATED IN SOUTHWESTERN Asia (mostly in the Anatolian peninsula) and in East Thrace in Southeastern Europe. Asian Turkey (made up largely of Anatolia), which includes 97 percent of the country, is separated from European Turkey by the Istanbul Bosporus, the Sea of Marmara, and the Dardanelles Bosporus (which together form a water link between the Black Sea and the Mediterranean). European Turkey (eastern Thrace or Rumelia in the Balkan peninsula) comprises 3 percent of the country.

Turkey's location at the crossroads of Europe and Asia makes it a country of significant geostrategic importance. Given its strategic location, large economy, and military strength, Turkey is a major regional power.

Turkey is divided into seven census regions: Marmara, Aegean, Black Sea, Central Anatolia, Eastern Anatolia, Southeastern Anatolia, and the Mediterranean. The uneven north Anatolian terrain running along the Black Sea resembles a long, narrow belt. This region comprises approximately one-sixth of Turkey's total land area. As a general trend, the inland Anatolian plateau becomes increasingly rugged as it progresses eastward.

Turkey's varied landscapes are the product of complex earth movements that have shaped the region over thousands of years and still manifest themselves in fairly frequent earthquakes and occasional volcanic eruptions. The Bosporus and the Dardanelles owe their existence to the fault lines running through Turkey that led to the creation of the Black Sea. There is an earthquake fault line across the north of the country from west to east, which caused a major earthquake in 1999. Mount Ararat is the highest peak in Turkey at 16,949 feet (5,166 m)

The occupation of Constantinople and Smyrna (Izmir) by the Allies in the aftermath of World War I prompted the establishment of the Turkish national movement. Under the leadership of Mustafa Kemal Atatürk Pasha, a military commander who had distinguished himself during the Battle of Gallipoli, the Turkish War of Independence was waged with the aim of revoking the terms of the Treaty of Sèvres.

By September 18, 1922, the occupying armies were expelled, and the new Turkish state was established. On November 1, the newly founded parliament formally abolished the Sultanate, thus ending 600 years of Ottoman rule. The Treaty of Lausanne of July 24, 1923, led to the international recognition of the sovereignty of the newly formed "Republic of Turkey" as the successor state of the Ottoman Empire, and the republic was officially proclaimed on October 29, 1923, in the new capital of Ankara.

Mustafa Kemal became the republic's first President and subsequently introduced many radical reforms with the aim of founding a new secular republic from the remnants of its Ottoman past. With the Surname Law of 1934, the Turkish Parliament bestowed upon Mustafa Kemal the honorific surname "Atatürk" ("Father of the Turks").

MARMARA REGION The Marmara Region, with a surface area of 25,869 square miles (67,000 square km), is the smallest but most densely populated of the seven geographical regions of Turkey. Densely populated, this area includes the cities of Istanbul and Edirne. It represents approximately 8.5 percent of the Turkish national territory and about 30 percent of its population. This region was officially put in existence after the Geography Congress of 1941 in Ankara and is geographically divided into four regional parts. Its name derives from the Sea of Marmara, which itself is named after the island of Marmara.

BLACK SEA REGION The Black Sea region has a steep, rocky coast with rivers that cascade through the gorges of the coastal ranges. A few larger rivers, those cutting back through the Pontic Mountains, have tributaries that flow in broad, elevated basins. Access inland from the coast is limited to a few narrow valleys because mountain ridges form an almost unbroken wall separating the coast from the interior. The higher slopes facing northwest tend to be densely forested. Because of these natural conditions, the Black Sea coast historically has been isolated from Anatolia.

An orange plantation in Dalaman, Turkey.

Running from Zonguldak in the west to Rize in the east, the narrow coastal strip widens at several places into fertile, intensely cultivated deltas. The Samsun area, close to the midpoint, is a major tobacco-growing region; east of it are numerous citrus groves. East of Samsun, the area around Trabzon is world-renowned for the production of hazelnuts, and farther east the Rize region has numerous tea plantations. All cultivable areas, including mountain slopes wherever they are not too steep, are sown or used as pasture. The mild, damp climate of the Black Sea coast makes commercial farming profitable. The western part of the Black Sea region, especially the Zonguldak area, is a center of coal mining and heavy industry.

AEGEAN REGION Located on the western side of Anatolia, the Aegean region has a fertile soil and a typically Mediterranean climate; with mild, wet winters and hot, dry summers. The broad, cultivated valley lowlands contain about half of the country's richest farmlands.

The largest city in the Aegean Region of Turkey is Izmir, which is also the country's third largest city and a major manufacturing center; as well as its second largest port after Istanbul.

Olive and olive oil production is particularly important for the economy of the region. The seaside town of Ayvalık and numerous towns in the provinces of Balıkesir, Izmir, and Aydın are particularly famous for their olive oil and related products; such as soap and cosmetics.

Shepherds with their animals near Tuz Gölü.

MEDITERRANEAN REGION Toward the east, the extensive plains around Adana, Turkey's fifth most populous city, consist largely of reclaimed flood lands. East of Adana, much of the coastal plain has limestone features such as collapsed caverns and sinkholes. Between Adana and Antalya, the Taurus Mountains rise sharply from the coast to high elevations. Other than Adana, Antalya, and Mersin, the Mediterranean coast has few major cities, although it has numerous farming villages.

CENTRAL ANATOLIA REGION Stretching inland from the Aegean coastal plain, the Central Anatolian occupies an area between the two zones of the folded mountains, extending east to the point where the two ranges converge. The plateau-like, semiarid highlands of Anatolia are considered the heartland of the country. The region varies in elevation from 1,969 to 3,937 feet (600 to 1,200 m) from west to east. The two largest basins on the plateau are the Konya Ovasi and the basin occupied by the large salt lake, Tuz Gölü. Both basins are characterized by inland drainage. Wooded areas are confined to the northwest and northeast of the plateau. Rain-fed cultivation is widespread, with wheat being the principal crop. Irrigated agriculture is restricted to the areas around rivers and wherever sufficient underground water is available.

EASTERN AND SOUTHEASTERN ANATOLIA REGIONS Eastern Anatolia, where the Pontus and Taurus mountain ranges converge, is rugged country with higher elevations, a more severe climate, and greater rainfall than on the Anatolian Plateau. The region is known as the Anti-Taurus, and the average elevation of its peaks exceeds 9,843 feet (3,000 m). Mount Ararat, at 16,949 feet (5,166 m), the highest point in Turkey, is located in the Anti-Taurus. Many of the Anti-Taurus peaks apparently are recently extinct volcanoes, to judge from extensive lava flows. Turkey's largest lake, Lake Van, is situated in the mountains at an elevation of 5,400 feet (1,646 m). The headwaters of three major rivers arise in the Anti-Taurus: the east-flowing Aras, which pours into the Caspian Sea; the south-flowing Euphrates; and the south-flowing Tigris, which eventually joins the Euphrates in Iraq before emptying into the Persian Gulf. Several small streams that empty into the Black Sea or landlocked Lake Van also originate in these mountains.

The economy of Turkey is largely developed, making Turkey one of the world's newly industrialized countries. The country is among the world's leading producers of agricultural products; textiles; motor vehicles, ships, and other transportation equipment; construction materials; consumer electronics and home appliances. Thanks to strict banking regulations, Turkey has emerged from the 2009 financial crisis relatively unscathed and not a cent of taxpayer's money has had to be spent bailing out Turkish banks.

Turkey has 10 United Nations Educational, Scientific and Cultural Organization (UNESCO) sites. Three interesting ones are the Hattusha, the archaeological site of Troy, and the Selimiye Mosque. Former capital of the Hittite empire, the archaeological site of Hattusha is notable for its urban organization, the types of construction that have been preserved (including the Lion Gate and the Royal Gate, and the ensemble of rock art at Yazilikaya. The city enjoyed considerable influence in Anatolia and northern Syria in the 2nd millennium B.C.

The archaeological site of Troy, with its 4,000 years of history, is one of the most famous sights in the world. The first excavations were undertaken by the famous archaeologist Heinrich Schliemann in 1870. In scientific terms, its extensive remains are the most significant demonstration of the first contact between the civilizations of Anatolia and the Mediterranean world. Moreover, the siege of Troy by Spartan and Achaean warriors from Greece in the 13th or 12th century B.C., immortalized by Homer in *The Iliad*, has inspired great creative artists throughout the world ever since.

The square-shaped Selimiye Mosque and its social complex—consisting of a single great dome and four slender minarets—dominates the skyline of the former Ottoman capital of Edirne. Sinan, the most famous of Ottoman architects in the 16th century, considered the complex, which includes madrasas (Islamic schools), a covered market, clock house, outer courtyard, and library, to be his best work. The interior decoration using Iznik tiles from the peak period of their production testifies to an art form that remains unsurpassed in this material. The complex is considered to be the most harmonious expression ever achieved of the Ottoman *külliye*, which is a group of buildings constructed around a mosque and then managed as a single institution.

GEOGRAPHY

Forest roses grow along the slopes of Borcka Artvin. Abounding in beautiful lakes and wild fields, some of the loveliest landscapes in the world are found in Turkey.

1

TURKEY LIES PARTLY IN EUROPE and partly in Asia. The European region, known as Thrace, is approximately 9,199 square miles (23,825 square km) in area. It is very small compared to the Asian region, called Anatolia, which measures about 293,342 square miles (759,752 square km).

The thermal spring waters of Pamukkale are renowned for their therapeutic powers. Laden with salt, these waters have calcified to form basins and dazzling white petrified cascades.

Turkey is one of the most earthquake-prone areas on earth because it sits on major geological fault lines. The North Anatolian Fault extends hundreds of miles from the Sea of Marmara in the western part of the country to the Eastern Anatolian highlands. The fault moves back and forth about 0.8 to 1 inches (2 to 2.5 cm) a year.

Dense pine forests cover the mountain slopes of the Kaçkar Mountains, part of the Pontic Mountains of Eastern Turkey.

Turkey is bordered by Greece and Bulgaria in the northwest, and the Aegean Sea to the west, Iran, Georgia, Azerbaijan, and Armenia to the east, and Iraq, Syria, and the Mediterranean Sea to the south. The Black Sea lies to the north. The European region of Turkey is separated from the Asian region by the Istanbul Bosporus Strait, the Sea of Marmara, and the Dardanelles Strait.

THE NATURAL ENVIRONMENT

The central mass of Turkey, known as the Central Anatolian Plateau, is surrounded by the Pontic Mountains to the north and the Taurus Mountains to the south. There are mountain ridges to the west and the east as well. Cut off from rain-bearing winds by mountain ranges, the central plateau is semiarid. The climate varies greatly, depending on geographical location. The Black Sea region to the north has a temperate climate with warm summers and mild winters. The western Aegean coastline and the southern Mediterranean shores are hot in summer, reaching temperatures of about 84°F (29°C). The western coast does not experience the freezing winters of the interior. Not surprisingly, tourists are attracted to the coastal regions where the average summer temperature is about 77°F (25°C).

The Bosporus is also known as the Istanbul Strait. It is the world's narrowest strait for international shipping.

THE BLACK SEA COAST

The Black Sea coast extends along the northern margins of the country, from the Bulgarian border in the west to Georgia in the east. Climatically, the whole area is influenced by the mountain ranges that lie just behind the thin coastal strip of land. Hot air moving over the coast rises to cross the mountains. But as it does, the higher altitude causes it to cool and fall as rain. Consequently, the Black Sea coast is the wettest part of Turkey. Only July and August are hot in this region.

Three of Europe's longest rivers flow into the Black Sea: the Don, the Dnieper, and the Danube. Powerful currents carry the waters through the Bosporus, the only outlet for the Black Sea. The Bosporus is a short strait, 19 miles (30 km) long, connecting the Black Sea with the Sea of Marmara.

The saline content of the water is very low in the area where the major rivers flow into the Black Sea. The salinity is half that of the Mediterranean Sea. However, in the southern part of the sea there is a vast underwater pool of salty, stagnant water that makes it difficult for marine life to survive.

The Pontic Mountains in this region follow the contour of the southern shore of the Black Sea. The slopes of the mountains that descend to the coast are covered in thick woods. Timber from this region is used to build

The village of Safranbolu in Zonguldak province is a good example of a 16th century Ottoman village that has remained intact over the years. The houses are half-timbered.

One of the chief tribes of the ancient kingdom of Colchis, the Laz were initially early adopters of Christianity, and most of them subsequently converted to Sunni Islam during Ottoman rule of the Caucasus in the 15th century.

houses and boats. Many of the villages in this region have a long tradition of building boats, which are used mainly for fishing but also provide a mode of transportation. Bays and natural harbors are rare along the coast. Due to the lack of safe harbors, people who make their living from the sea are skilled in handling small boats in rough weather.

The mountains have also served to make this part of Turkey isolated and inaccessible. Until very recently, contact with the rest of Turkey was minimal, and as a result various Turkish ethnic groups, such as the Laz, have managed to survive culturally intact over generations.

These ethnic groups are heavily dependent on agriculture for a livelihood. Crops such as hazelnuts and cherries, tea, and tobacco are commonly cultivated. Major tea plantations are found in the Trabzon region.

In the past, mineral deposits around the region of Sinop on the coast attracted adventurers and entrepreneurs. Jason and the Argonauts, the legendary explorers, travelled to this part of Turkey in search of the Golden Fleece and valuable minerals. Today, it is said that villagers still place sheepskins in the streams hoping to collect traces of gold dust.

Ölüdeniz, or the Blue Lagoon, in Fethiye stands at the point where the Aegean and Mediterranean seas meet. Abounding in beautiful beaches and olive groves, the Aegean coast has one of the loveliest landscapes in Turkey.

THE AEGEAN REGION

The Aegean region, extending from the Dardanelles in the north to the Greek island of Rhodes in the south, is one of the most beautiful regions of Turkey. The area has attracted visitors for centuries. Indeed, many visitors now come to this part of Turkey to see the treasures of the ancient Greek and Roman civilizations. Tourists also come to enjoy the summer sun, splendid beaches, and beautiful resorts and villages.

Long ago, geography attracted outsiders to this part of Turkey. The plains inland from the Aegean coast form some of the most fertile land in the country. Many of Turkey's export crops, such as olives, tobacco, grapes, and figs, flourish in the hospitable climate and accommodating soil.

The main cities in the Aegean region are Izmir, Manisa, and Aydin.

THE MEDITERRANEAN REGION

Turkey's Mediterranean region extends from Rhodes to the Syrian coast. This region is dominated by mountains. Along the extreme western Mediterranean coast, the Taurus Mountains make the area largely inaccessible to those without a boat or yacht. The fine scenery, beautiful beaches, and warm, turquoise water gives this area the name Turquoise Coast.

The mountains near the Mediterranean city of Olimpos are known for an interesting natural phenomenon. The rocks found in this area release methane gas, which produces burning flames when it comes into contact with oxygen in the air.

Along the Turquoise Coast are two of the Seven Wonders of the Ancient World—the ruins of the Mausoleum of Maussollos in Halicarnassus and the remains of the Temple of Artemis in Ephesus.

The famous old harbor in Antalya. The area around Antalya is called the Turkish Riviera because of its beautiful beaches and warm Mediterranean climate. Situated on top of cliffs overlooking a crescent-shaped bay, Antalya is the area's chief tourist destination.

The beautiful Kaputas Beach in Anatolia.

Oil technologists have studied these burning flames, hoping that it would lead them to large deposits of oil, but only traces of methane have been detected so far. The phenomenon—called chimera—is named after a fire-breathing female monster in Greek mythology. The chimera has a head of a lion, the body of a she-goat, and the tail of a dragon and was once believed to inhabit these mountains.

In the area around the port of Antalya, the Taurus Mountains do not extend to the sea. Instead, a fertile plain here has helped development in the region around the port, while the sunny climate and unspoiled beaches attract visitors by the thousands.

To the east of Antalya, mountains again predominate. In the past, this area was renowned for its dangerous shores and pirates. Farther along the southern side of the mountains is the vast plain of Cilicia. This is now a prosperous area in Turkey, largely due to its production of cotton.

ANATOLIA

Anatolia includes the Central Anatolian Plateau and the eastern and southeastern parts of Turkey that have no coastline.

Central Anatolia is a forbidding mixture of desert and grasslands, hot in summer and freezing in winter. Hardy goats and sheep graze on the rocky soil, but nearly all the arable land is used to grow grain. Water is often scarce during the summer months, except in areas where irrigation has been introduced.

In the south, a distinctive feature of the landscape is the number of lakes lying between mountains. A high salt content and the ever-present danger of flooding have discouraged communities from forming near these lakes. Nevertheless, people have lived in central Anatolia for millions of years.

Southeastern Anatolia is a barren plateau drained by the Tigris and Euphrates rivers. The dry land is hard to cultivate, resulting in a largely

rural and underdeveloped region. In 1976 the Turkish government initiated an extensive dam-building project called the Southeastern Anatolia Project (Güneydogu Anadolu Projesi) or GAP to irrigate the land and make it fit for growing crops. Since its implementation in 1976, the project has made steady progress, and the Turkish government aims to transform the region into a major agricultural center. Due to irrigation from the Atatürk Dam, harvest yields of cotton, wheat, barley, lentils, and other grains in the Harran plain have tripled. A number of Agriculture Department backed initiatives are encouraging farmers to experiment with new varieties of fruits, vegetables, and nuts that did not exist in the region prior. As a result of GAP, land values, personal income, and the number of agricultural and personal vehicles have increased in the past eight years.

Southeastern Anatolia is also home to the famous tomb and temple complex of Nemrut Dagi, whose stones have been sculptured into human heads and figures.

Eastern Anatolia is the largest and least populated region of Turkey. The heart of this rural region is Lake Van (Van Gölü), covering 1,434 square miles (3,714 square km). Eastern Anatolia is also home to inactive volcanoes.

A view of the hilly terrain and meadows of Eastern Anatolia.

The fairy chimneys of Cappadocia served as dwellings for the region's early inhabitants. Homes were carved out from the soft stone.

CAPPADOCIA

The unique landscape of Cappadocia is the result of volcanic eruptions that occurred millions of years ago. The eruptions covered hundreds of square miles of land with a layer of volcanic ash, which became compressed to form a porous rock known as tuff. Three volcanoes were responsible for the phenomenon, and their peaks are still a visible feature of the region today.

Tuff varies in hardness. Tuff is generally soft and easily eroded by water. However, some layers of tuff contain harder substances such as basalt and ignimbrite. When rainwater flows down tuff-covered hills and plateaus, the softer tuff layers erode, leaving the harder layers intact. Over centuries, this steady erosion produced a landscape of conical pillars capped by boulders. The boulder cap is made of the harder, more resistant rock and rests on soft tuff pillars. These formations are known as fairy chimneys, and some can reach a height of 130 feet (40 m). Wind erosion also contributes to the thinning of these tuff pillars. Further thinning causes a fairy chimney to eventually collapse.

The underground cities of Cappadocia are believed to date from the 4th century A.D.. They were constructed primarily as storage spaces for the Hittite population, but were later used by Christians escaping persecution by the Romans. They adapted these spaces to be used as homes, schools, and churches. Some parts of the subterranean cities are open to the public.

The original ventilation system is still adequate to allow groups of tourists to explore the remains 262 feet (80 m) below the ground. Stables, wine cellars, and churches are still recognizable. One room that may have functioned as a schoolroom or communal dining area contains two large, stone-cut tables. A complex series of channels connects the many floor levels, with the deeper levels containing the dungeons. Extraordinary tunnels and passageways have been discovered leading from the cities, one running a distance of nearly 6 miles (10 km) underground. Forty underground cities have been found, of which the largest is Derinkuyu (above).

The soft property of the tuff enabled the region's early people to carve dwellings or hiding places within the region's hills and valleys. Byzantine churches and monasteries were found in the area. The most famous churches are those in the Ihara Valley. Even more spectacular are the underground cities that have been carved out of the rock, some of which extend many levels underground. These underground cities were probably built to accommodate a large number of people and their domestic animals for long periods of time.

Mount Ararat is
also known as
Aghri Dagh in
Turkish, which
means Mountain
of the Ark.

THE MOUNTAIN OF NOAH

The most famous mountain in this country of mountains is not noted for its height but rather for what is believed to once have landed on its summit.

Mount Ararat, rising to 16,949 feet (5,166 m), is Turkey's highest mountain and is believed to be the mountain on which Noah's Ark came to rest after the great flood subsided. It is situated close to the border with Iran (formerly Persia), and the Iranian name for the mountain is Koh-i-Nuh, the Mountain of Noah.

Ararat is an inactive volcanic mountain with two peaks—Great Ararat and Little Ararat—that are separated by a distance of 7 miles (11 km). Snow is found almost year-round on the higher slopes, while most of the lower slopes are pasture land.

This region of Turkey was once inhabited by Armenians. According to Armenian clerics, the mountain is a sacred place for the Armenian people. It was not until the early 19th century that anyone was allowed to climb to the summit. In 1829 German explorer Johann Jacob Frederick von Parrot became the first person to reach Ararat's summit. Since then, Ark hunters, geologists, and mountaineers have scaled Ararat's beautiful, pristine terrain.

ANKARA

Ankara has been the capital of Turkey since 1923. In ancient times, Ankara was the site of an important settlement. It was a trading center during the Hittite civilization and was known as Ancyra. It was occupied by the Romans, Persians, Seljuk Turks, and the Crusaders. The Seljuks renamed it Angora. In 1923 when Kemal Atatürk, the founder of modern Turkey, chose to establish the nation's capital here, Ankara was only a small provincial town. The pace of development has been so fast that the city's borders have stretched to the surrounding hills, and the metropolis is still growing. The city's name was changed to Ankara in 1930.

Ankara's population is now 4.96 million. During the harsh Anatolian winter, thick smog covers the city. The smog is a result of the extensive burning of coal to warm houses and offices for the city's large population. In the summer's intense heat, a dusty haze often surrounds the city. The pollution in Ankara has reached dangerous levels in the past.

An aerial view of Ankara. In addition to being the seat of government and the administrative capital, Ankara is also Turkey's second-most important industrial city.

As the administrative center of the country, Ankara serves as the headquarters for important businesses in the nation. The unemployed, lured by the city's success, come to the capital in search of work and consequently add to the city's growing number of shantytowns. The problem has increased over the years, with temporary dwellings becoming permanent residences. The authorities, realizing they cannot expel thousands of families, have provided these areas with electricity and fresh water. Many of the slums in Ankara have been replaced by housing projects in the form of tower blocks.

ISTANBUL

Istanbul is the only city in the world that straddles two continents: Europe and Asia. The city is a surprise to many people, especially visitors from North America and Western Europe. It is mostly in Europe but yet has a distinctly Asian feel. Istanbul has a population of 13.85 million, three times more than Ankara. Although Istanbul is no longer the nation's capital, it is Turkey's cultural, economic, and financial center.

Istanbul is full of historic and cultural treasures. The city skyline is shaped by domes and minarets. Two of its most famous buildings highlight the city's rich and varied past. Ayasofya (Hagia Sophia), also known as the Church of

Istanbul's skyline and ferries. Istanbul is the only city in the world built on two continents. It stands on the shores of the Bosporus, where the waters of the Black Sea mingle with those of the Sea of Marmara and the Golden Horn, a narrow channel off the Bosporus.

the Holy Wisdom, was built in the sixth century and represents the Byzantine Christian era. The Blue Mosque of Sultan Ahmet bears testimony to the time when Istanbul was under the control of the powerful Ottomans who made it the capital of the Islamic empire.

Istanbul has seen the rise and fall of powerful empires, having been the capital of the Roman, Byzantine, and Ottoman empires. The city's name has changed from Byzantium, Nova Roma, Constantinople, Konstantiniye, and finally, Istanbul throughout its history.

Istanbul is a bustling city, with roads, bridges, trains, boats, and planes bringing in travelers from other parts of Turkey and the world. Its official population is about 18 percent of the country's total population. Due to the rapid growth of population, Istanbul is becoming overcrowded. The city suffers from traffic congestion and air pollution. The lack of infrastructure to support the increase in city dwellers has made these problems worse. As a result of Istanbul's exponential growth during the 20th century, a significant portion of the city's outskirts is comprised of slums. At present, some slums are being gradually demolished and replaced by modern mass-housing compounds, like in Ankara. Istanbul is facing problems similar to many modern cities around the world, but its ancient charm remains.

INTERNET LINKS

http://kids.nationalgeographic.com/kids/places/find/turkey/

Fascinating bite-sized facts on the geography of Turkey with lovely pictures from National Geographic Kids.

www.atozkidsstuff.com/turkey.html

Interesting facts about Turkey with links to maps, pictures, folk tales, and fun facts.

http://countries.pppst.com/turkey.html

Free Powerpoint presentations done by kids all around the world about Turkey.

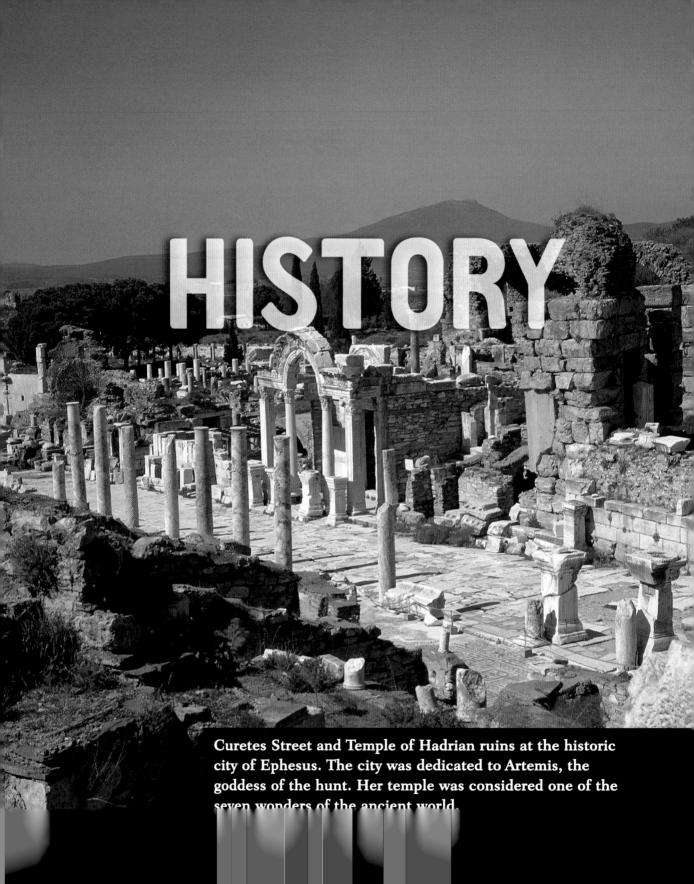

HISTORY

Curetes Street and Temple of Hadrian ruins at the historic city of Ephesus. The city was dedicated to Artemis, the goddess of the hunt. Her temple was considered one of the seven wonders of the ancient world.

2

T URKEY HAS A RICH AND illustrious past, predating the arrival of the Turks in the 11th century. The early Turks called the land Anatolia, which is derived from its Greek name Anatole, meaning sunrise or the East.

Little is known about the earliest inhabitants, but evidence of human existence in the region dates back to 9000 B.C. The first civilization in what is now Turkey was that of the Hittites. Many more civilizations followed.

The first Turkic people lived in a region extending from Central Asia to Siberia with the majority of them living in China historically.

A recreation of the Roman Bas-Reliefs at Ephesus by artist Gaetano Mercati.

THE HITTITES

The Hittite empire (1900 to 1300 B.C.) was one of the first and most significant settlements in Turkey. The Hittites' center of power was in central Anatolia at Hattusas, near present-day Ankara. The empire collapsed in 1200 B.C., and was followed by a succession of small states, among the most important of which were Phrygia and Lydia.

Excavations at Hattusas suggest that the Hittite city was enormous. The fortified wall enclosing the city was about 2 miles (3.3 km) long. The Hittites were also an advanced civilization with a professional army. They built majestic temples and developed their own distinctive architecture and figurative art as well. A recurring symbol of Hittite art is a lion with an open mouth, found on many Hittite art pieces, statues, and carvings.

At the height of their power, the Hittites were comparable to the ancient Egyptians. The Hittites treated men and women equally, gave slaves certain rights, ruled with an advanced system of government, and had a policy restraining the torture and mutilation of prisoners of war. Their advanced society distinguished them from their contemporaries in the Middle East.

The Hittite Rock Sanctuary in Yasilikaya. Hittite architecture was highly original; they built magnificent temples and developed a figurative art that was to be widespread in Anatolia.

THE GREEKS AND THE PERSIANS

By 900 B.C., Greeks had crossed the Aegean Sea and settled along the western shores of Anatolia. Greek colonies at Troy, Ephesus, and Miletus became commercial centers.

By 700 B.C., however, most of the Greek colonies had fallen under Lydian rule. Although the Lydians allowed the Greeks to retain their own government and institutions, they imposed hefty taxes on all the Greek communities. Croesus (560—546 B.C.), the last king of Lydia, was known for his vast wealth, an indication of the extent of Lydian power. Such wealth and power soon attracted envy. In 546 B.C. the Persians under Cyrus the Great conquered the Lydian empire. The Persians ruled the Greek cities in the region for several centuries. It was not until Alexander the Great conquered Anatolia in 334 B.C. that the Greeks were able to fully regain their influence.

THE INFLUENCE OF ROME

After the death of Alexander the Great, Anatolia was divided among various Greek generals and later reunited under the Seleucid and Attalid dynasties. The last of the Attalid kings gave the region to the Romans in A.D. 43. In A.D. 330

Known to the world through Homer's ancient Greek epics, The Iliad *and* The Odyssey, *Troy is very much a part of the history of Turkey. The ancient city is located in northwestern Anatolia.*

The remains of Troy (Truva in Turkish) are not as spectacular as its history. According to Homer, the war between the Trojans and the Greeks came about after Paris, the son of the king of Troy, abducted Helen, the queen of the Greek city of Sparta. Her irate husband, Menelaus, gathered a host of Greek heroes to help him recover his wife. Achilles and Odysseus are the best known of these heroes. Under the leadership of King Agamemnon, they sailed off to Troy. After 10 years of fighting, the wily Odysseus devised a plan to trick the Trojans with a hollow wooden horse (below) in which the Greeks entered the city.

Today, what is left of the walls testifies to a city that was once thought only to exist in the imagination of ancient storytellers. Legend became reality in 1871 with the findings of Heinrich Schliemann, a German archeologist who excavated in northwestern Turkey. Schliemann uncovered nine layers of the city, each layer representing a separate stage in the city's evolution. The oldest stage dates back to 3600 B.C., while the last layer was built during the time of the Roman Empire. Troy VII, which corresponds to the seventh period in the history of the city, was destroyed by fire around 1250 B.C. and is believed to have been the city of King Priam described in The Iliad.

the Roman emperor Constantine made the Greek city of Byzantium the center of his eastern empire, renaming it Constantinople, which in Greek means city of Constantine. When Rome fell to the Goths in A.D. 476, Constantinople became the capital of the Roman Empire. Anatolia was added to the growing Roman Empire in the seventh century and flourished under Roman control. During this time, Christianity was introduced to Anatolia by the apostle Paul, a Jew from Tarsus in Cilicia. In A.D. 532 the construction of the Ayasofya (Hagia Sophia) church in Constantinople began under the order of the Roman emperor Justinian.

An artist's recreation of the walled city of Constantinople.

THE COMING OF THE TURKS

The early Turks were from central Asia. They migrated or were driven west from their homeland by the Mongols.

In the eighth century, Turks came into contact with Muslims from the Middle East. By the 10th century, the Turks had adopted the Islamic faith and were united under the rule of the Karahans. This was a time of progress and commercial enterprise. Mosques, inns, schools, and bridges were built along the many caravan routes, known as the Silk Road, which went through the Middle East on to China.

In 1040 the Seljuk Turks rose to power and established an empire. They introduced the Turkish language to the region. In 1071, in a major battle at Malazgirt in eastern Anatolia, the remnants of the Byzantine army were defeated, marking the beginning of Muslim Turkish influence in Anatolia.

The Seljuks introduced Islam to the mainly Christian region. In 1092 the conversion of the people from Christianity to Islam led Pope Urban II to wage a war against the Seljuks. This was the beginning of the First Crusade. In time, another three Crusades were to take place, bringing much bloodshed and conflict to the region.

The western part of Anatolia, along with the Black Sea and Mediterranean coasts, remained as a Byzantine territory, while the Turkish Seljuk Empire developed its own cultural identity in the heart of Anatolia. The Seljuk Empire came to an end in the 13th century, after it was conquered by invading Mongol forces.

By the 1330s, Mongol power had weakened, and Anatolia was broken into smaller principalities. One such principality became powerful under the leadership of Osman I, founder of the Osmanli dynasty, known in Europe as the Ottoman Empire.

A painting depicting the Victorious Turks entering Constantinople, making it the Ottoman Empire capital in 1453.

THE OTTOMAN EMPIRE

The Ottoman Empire grew through conquest, purchase, and marriage. At the height of its power, the Ottoman Empire included most of North Africa, Iraq, and large areas of Eastern Europe, as well as Islam's holy cities of Mecca and Medina.

In 1453 Mehmet II (Muhammad II) launched a fifty-day siege against Constantinople. Victorious, he renamed the city Istanbul, which comes from the Greek phrase "*eis tin polin*", which means to the city.

In 1529, the empire experienced its first major defeat when it failed to capture Vienna, the capital of the Hapsburg empire. This halted the Ottoman Empire's westward expansion. From the 17th century onward, the Ottoman Empire gradually declined, finally breaking up in 1918, at the end of World War I. The empire had lasted more than 600 years.

THE OTTOMAN SULTANS

The Ottoman Sultans invariably earned themselves epithets. After the fall of Constantinople, Mehmed II became known as the Conqueror. During his reign, the church of Ayasofya (Hagia Sophia) was converted to a mosque, and Istanbul replaced Baghdad as the center for Sunni Islam. However, Istanbul remained the center for the Greek Orthodox Church, since Mehmed II believed he was a successor of the Byzantine emperors and therefore a protector of the Greek Orthodox Church. Mehmed II's son, Bayezid II, who succeeded to the throne, was called the Pious because of his works of charity. Bayezid II was eventually deposed by his own son, who was more aggressive and earned the title of Selim the Grim. Under Süleyman the Magnificent, the Ottoman Empire reached the height of its power. Art, architecture, and literature flourished.

Süleyman the Magnificent was known not only for his military campaigns, but also for his achievements in the fields of law, literature, art, and architecture.

The Ottoman Empire had no constitutional system for choosing a new sultan. For centuries, it was the practice of any new sultan to commit mass fratricide. All of the sultan's brothers would be immediately killed in an attempt to prevent any rival claims to the throne. Such practices contributed to the West's image of the Ottomans as an uncivilized empire.

Other than the Janissaries, the sultans did not force Islam on their subjects. When walled cities were conquered, non-Muslim communities simply withdrew to the suburbs.

THE JANISSARIES

In the 14th century, as the Ottoman Empire began taking over Christian lands, a practice developed wherein Christian boys were captured and raised as elite Muslim corps. Called Janissaries from the Turkish word yeniçeri *(yen-uh-CHAY-RUH) which means new troops, they were trained as warriors, and those showing talent were groomed for administrative positions. For many years, freeborn Muslims were not eligible to join this privileged group. It was not until the 17th century, after the population declined due to wars against Austria and Persia, that Muslims were granted membership. At the height of their influence, the Janissaries were involved in deposing sultans and creating new ones.*

MUSTAFA KEMAL ATATÜRK

When World War I broke out in 1914, the Ottoman Empire joined the Central Powers consisting of Germany, Austria-Hungary, and Bulgaria. The defeat of the Central Powers in 1918 was a final blow to the declining Ottoman Empire. In 1919 the country was placed under the control of European Allied occupational forces. This sparked Turkish resentment, and a resistance movement arose. This movement was led by the Turkish military hero Mustafa Kemal Atatürk.

The escalation in fighting finally led to the war for independence. A victorious Turkish resistance drove the occupational forces out of their country and abolished the Ottoman Sultanate. In 1923 a peace treaty set the boundaries of the new Republic of Turkey, and Atatürk was elected Turkey's first president.

Atatürk initiated many reforms to the system of law and government. One new law required Turks to have surnames. He was therefore honored with the surname Atatürk, which means Father of the Turks.

Atatürk was born in 1881 in the Ottoman city of Saloniki, now in present-day Greece. He was given the name *Kemal*, which means perfection, by his mathematics teacher for his academic excellence. In 1905 he graduated from the Military Academy and served in the Ottoman army, winning many victories for them. He led the Turkish resistance during the fighting in the Gallipoli Peninsula between the Turks and the Allied forces.

Mustafa Kemal Atatürk died in November 1938. He is remembered for his social and political changes to modernize and secularize Turkey during his presidency. He is greatly revered today, and it is considered illegal to criticize him.

Mustafa Kemal Atatürk, Father of the Turks. Ataturk had distinguished himself as a military commander in the Gallipoli campaign in World War I.

SECULARIZATION

As president of Turkey from 1923 to 1938, Atatürk supervised an extraordinary reform of his country. He was driven by a desire to assert Turkey's identity as a modern secular state. Above all, he was determined to dissociate the state from Islam. This meant implementing the Gregorian calendar to replace the Islamic lunar one in 1923 and replacing Islamic law with statutes resembling the European legal system. The Turkish Constitution is modeled after the Swiss Constitution.

At a social level, Atatürk outlawed polygamy, and women were given the right to vote. Both marriage and divorce became matters for the civil courts rather than religious issues. In 1928 Atatürk replaced the traditional Ottoman-Arabic script with a romanized alphabet to enable better communication between Turkey and the West.

A big rally by the ruling AK Party in Zeytinburnu, Istanbul

AFTER WORLD WAR II

After World War II, Turkey went through a prolonged period of political instability and was controlled by a succession of military governments. In 1945 Turkey joined the United Nations (UN) and was a founding member of the Organization for Economic Cooperation and Development (OECD). Turkey also participated in the Korean War, and in 1952 became a member of the North Atlantic Treaty Organization (NATO). The country today is still the only Muslim member of NATO.

In 1974 the Greek island of Cyprus, home to a minority Turkish population, was invaded by Turkish troops seeking to protect their interests. Conflict between the Greeks and the Turks led the UN to step in to help resolve the conflict, which continued to strain Turkish-Greek relations into the 21st century. A peaceful settlement to the problem is critical for Turkey as it waits to join the EU.

Civilian rule was reestablished in Turkey in 1983, but many problems remained. The Kurdish population struggled for independence for years and human rights violations became commonplace. Elections in November 2002 installed a new government headed by the Adalet ve Kalkinmai (AK), or Justice and Development, party led by a former mayor of Istanbul, Recep Tayyip Erdogan. AK Party won the 2007 elections and in the general elections held on June 12, 2011, the AK Party further increased its share of the popular vote to 49.8 percent and secured 327 parliamentary seats to form a third-consecutive majority government. A large part of the population has welcomed the marking of an end to the political and economic instability all too often present during the 1990s.

ARMENIAN GENOCIDE

The Armenian Genocide refers to the premeditated extermination of the Armenian people of the Ottoman Empire, which reached its peak during

Turkey supports the war on terrorism and has been an important ally of the United States in its anti-terrorism efforts.

World War I. It was carried out by the Turkish government and involved the torture and killing of large numbers of Armenians.

Between 1915 and 1918, it is believed that more than one million Armenians disappeared. Many of them were left to die in the Syrian Desert. Today, Armenians are seeking a formal acknowledgment of this crime based on the UN Convention of the Prevention and Punishment of the Crime of Genocide. Official Turkish history, however, does not document any such genocide against the Armenian people. Turkey has rejected the evidence based on their collection of facts that they have used to refute the allegations. The issue has not been resolved. The Armenian community commemorates the genocide on April 24 each year.

Activists gather to mark the anniversary of the massacre of Armenians during World War I. The total number of resulting Armenian deaths is generally held to have been between 1-1.5 million.

INTERNET LINKS

www.guardian.co.uk/flash/0,,1316326,00.html

A very interesting and interactive flash website on the history of Turkey from *The Guardian*.

www.historyworld.net/wrldhis/PlainTextHistories.asp?historyid=ac94

A detailed history of Turkey that makes for a very fun read.

www.lonelyplanet.com/turkey/history#227660

A comprehensive history of Turkey from the Lonely Planet Travel Guide broken up with hyperlinks.

GOVERNMENT

A statue of Mustafa Kemal Atatürk in Ulus Square, Ankara. Turkey's first president, Atatürk laid the groundwork for the transformation of Turkey into a modern state.

3

TURKEY'S MODERN DEMOCRATIC system of government has existed since 1983, when the army permitted a general election after a military takeover in 1980. The possibility of another military coup occurring is remote. It is more likely that Turkey will retain its democratic institutions and become more liberal.

During the Cold War, the country was supported by the West as a bulwark against the Soviet Union. Today, a confidence is emerging among the country's leaders, and pressure from Islamic fundamentalists is being contained.

Turkey is a republic with an elected president, appointed prime minister, and a Grand National Assembly. The government is administered centrally and locally.

The present government is led by the Adalet ve Kalkinmai (AK) party. In the 2002 elections, the party's Islamic roots were a cause for concern among voters, who had fears that the AK party would threaten Turkey's secular constitution. Turkish women, in particular, were concerned that the party could restrict the equal rights they enjoy today. Historically, the party opposed the policy prohibiting women working in the government and education sectors from wearing headscarves to work.

The AK party has reassured the Turkish people of its stand for democratic freedoms and human rights. Much remains to be seen, but the world is looking to Turkey to possibly become the first country to integrate Islam and Western democracy in its system of government.

The President
of Turkey is the
head of state who
holds a largely
ceremonial role but
with substantial
reserve powers.

PROPORTIONAL REPRESENTATION

Turkey's electoral system elects members of parliament according to the proportion of votes they attract rather than the actual number of votes they receive. Proportional representation goes hand in hand with multimember constituencies, meaning that there may be three or four candidates elected for just one seat in the parliament, depending on the proportion of votes each party receives. The traditional argument against proportional representation is that it allows many minority parties to win seats and thus decreases the chances of forming a government with a clear majority of seats.

Turkey has modified its version of proportional representation in order to deal with this problem. In Turkey, a party must attain 10 percent of the national vote before it can be considered for a seat in the parliament. For example, in a four-seat constituency, a party must win 25 percent of the vote, in a three-seat constituency, 33 percent, and so on. The AK government formed after the 2011 elections won a clear majority of seats in the parliament, 327 out of 550 seats, with 49.8 percent of the votes, thereby resuming their one-party rule after the 1987 to 2002 coalition government. The next presidential election is due to be held in 2014, within the end of term for the incumbent president. It will be the first election where the voters, instead of Parliament, elects the president.

THE ARMY

The army has intervened in the process of government on three separate occasions, in 1960, 1971, and 1980. Each coup was followed by a voluntary return to parliamentary democracy and civilian order restored to the country. The Turkish army protects Turkey's democracy. The army sees itself as the guardian of the secular reforms introduced by Atatürk and keeps Islamic fundamentalism in check, upholding Atatürk's separation of religion and state. This means that any political party, including the governing AK party, comes under the army's scrutiny.

The Turkish Armed Forces is the second-largest standing armed force in the North Atlantic Treaty Organization (NATO), after the U.S. Armed Forces, with a combined strength of just over a million uniformed personnel serving in its five branches. Since 2003, Turkey contributes military personnel to European Military Exercises. Turkey is also considered to be the strongest

A constitution introduced on November 7 1982 gave Turkey's Grand National Assembly legislative power over the country. The Grand National Assembly consists of two chambers, the National Assembly and the Senate. The Grand National Assembly convenes on the first day of September every year.

The president, who wields the executive power of the state, is elected for a five-year term. The president has the power to appoint a prime minister and to dissolve the Grand National Assembly.

military power of the Middle East region besides Israel. The military has been important in controlling Kurdish violence in Turkey. The army also plays a role as an anti-terrorist force in eastern Turkey.

When male citizens reach 20 years of age, they are required to serve 18 months of military service in the Turkish army.

HUMAN RIGHTS

There have been serious allegations of violations of human rights in Turkey. In 1987, after a storm of Western protest, Turkey agreed to lift all martial laws and to release some of its many political prisoners. The government soon came under fire again for approving the death penalty for political prisoners in 1989 and 1993.

The country has made significant improvements in addressing its human rights issues, but many serious problems remain. One aspect of human rights abuse is the use of torture by Turkish security forces to interrogate detainees. Reports of torture leading to death are widespread. Detainees are also held for long periods of time and do not have easy access to an attorney. Prison conditions are also poor. Turkey does not tolerate terrorism, and the penalties are harsh for anyone the government considers a terrorist.

The Turkish Army deposed the first democratically elected Prime Minister of Turkey, Adnan Menderes, and executed him, as they feared the ideals of Atatürk were in danger.

2003 ISTANBUL BOMBINGS

The 2003 Istanbul bombings were two truck bomb attacks carried out on November 15, 2003 in Istanbul, Turkey, leaving 63 people dead, and 750 wounded. Several men have been convicted for their involvement. On November 15, 2003, two trucks carrying bombs slammed into the Beth Israel Synagogues and Neve Shalom synagogues in Istanbul and exploded. The explosions devastated the synagogues and killed 30 people, most of them Turkish Muslims and injured more than 300 others. Six Jews were among the dead. After the 2003 Istanbul Bombings were linked to Al-Qaeda (an international terrorist organization), Turkey deployed troops to Afghanistan to fight Taliban forces and Al-Qaeda operatives, with the hopes of dismantling both groups. Turkey's responsibilities include providing security in Kabul (it currently leads Regional Command Capital), as well as in Wardak Province.

THE KURDS

The Kurds make up 18 percent of Turkey's population. Their feelings of persecution have led to frequent clashes with the government and a bid for separation from Turkey.

A separatist movement, called the Kurdish Workers Party, or Partiya Karkeren Kurdistan (PKK), was formed in 1978, which struggled for an independent Kurdish state in southeastern Turkey. This led to acts of violence on both sides, and the Kurdish issue dominated Turkish politics for years thereafter. During the 1980s and 1990s many Kurdish rural communities were uprooted in an effort to limit the PKK's base of logistical support. The PKK is listed as a terrorist organization by Turkey, the United States, and the European Union.

The government's treatment of the Kurdish population has also been the subject of severe criticism in Turkey and around the world. Turkish Kurds have been subjected to strong assimilationist pressure from the Turkish government. The government, the Kurds claim, is trying to deprive them of their Kurdish identity by referring to them as Mountain Turks and banning traditional Kurdish festivals and dress. Such allegations are seen as a stumbling block to Turkey's entry into the EU. The government defends itself

Turkey has a constitutional court, whose function is to rule on the constitutional nature of laws passed by the parliament. Other court cases are handled by a council of state and a court of appeals.

by claiming that the criticisms refer only to isolated cases and that attempts are being made to redress such wrongs.

As a step toward aligning Turkey with EU standards and practices, the Turkish government abolished the death penalty in 2002. New laws were also passed to guarantee the right of minority groups, including the Kurds, to use their own languages in schools and in the mass media. The laws on censorship were relaxed, giving the media greater freedom of expression, while the laws governing the practices of the police were tightened.

The leader of the Kurds, Abdullah Öcalan, was captured in Kenya on February 16, 1999. He is currently in prison. In 2010, after PKK rebels killed five Turkish soldiers in a series of incidents in eastern and southeastern Turkey, several locations in Iraqi Kurdistan were attacked by the Turkish Air Force early in June 2010. Violent Kurdish protests erupted from March to July 2011 in Turkey and Kurdish supporters overseas.

Kurds attending the annual **Newroz** political rally in Diyarbakir. The Kurds live in an area spread over several countries, including Iran, Iraq, and Turkey.

INTERNET LINKS

www.guardian.co.uk/world/interactive/2011/dec/29/kurdistan-kurds-turkey-iran-iraq-interactive?intcmp=239

An interactive timeline from *Guardian* describing the 2011 Kurdish conflict in Turkey.

www.globalfirepower.com/country-military-strength-detail.asp?country_id=Turkey

This website gives details on the Turkish military strength.

www.meforum.org/2160/turkey-military-catalyst-for-reform

An interesting argument from the *Middle East Quarterly* about how Turkey's military has protected freedom in Turkey.

ECONOMY

Headquarters of the Türkiye İş Bankası in Levent, Istanbul. İş bank is Turkey's first public bank and premiere national financial institution.

4

TURKEY HAS COME OUT of the global economic crisis relatively better off than many other emerging economies. Partly thanks to tough regulation, not a single Turkish bank has gone under.

That is also because, unlike many Western banks, they have few toxic assets and limited mortgage exposure. So the government has not had to divert taxpayers' money into rescuing banks.

In 2009, the Turkish Government introduced various economic stimulus measures to reduce the impact of the financial crisis such as temporary tax cuts on automobiles, home appliances, and housing. As a result, the production of durable consumer goods increased by 7.2 percent, despite a decrease in automotive production.

Automatic teller machines in Turkey.

The Turkish Stock Market and credit rating agencies have responded positively. According to *The Economist*, share prices in Turkey nearly doubled over the course of 2009. On 8 January 2010, International credit rating agency Moody's upgraded Turkey's rating with a notch. Moody's upgraded Turkey's Government Bond Rating from Ba3 to Ba2. Turkey is one of the few countries that saw its rating upgraded by two notches.

NEW LINKS

While Turkey remains wholeheartedly committed to joining the EU, the country also forges economic links with its eastern neighbors. This process first began in the 1990s after the collapse of the Soviet Union and is being reinvigorated under the AK government. One major development is the Baku-Ceyhan oil pipeline from Azerbaijan to Turkey. The first oil that was pumped from the Baku end of the pipeline on 10 May 2005 reached Ceyhan on 28 May 2006 as the oil had to travel under the Caspian Sea. Another project brings a supply of Russian natural gas to Turkey. Russian natural gas accounts for 65 percent of Turkey's natural gas needs. The supply of natural gas has been increasing since the opening of the 249-mile (400-km) Blue Stream pipeline in 2003.

Turkey has close economic and cultural links with Azerbaijan. There is also the possibility of closer economic ties with Armenia, a country with which it

Turkish President Ahmet Necdet Sezer (*left*) shakes hand with Samuel Bodman as Georgian President Mikhail Saakashvili (*second from left*) watches and Azeri President Ilham Aliyev (right) applauds during an opening ceremony of Baku-Tbilisi-Ceyhan pipeline.

Turkey was first considered as a candidate for EU membership in 1999. In early 2003, the EU assured Turkey that serious talks on entry would begin at the end of 2005, provided Turkey made a number of reforms in the areas of civil and human rights, especially the right of free speech. Turkey was also under an obligation to reduce the role of the military in political affairs and improve cultural rights for the Kurds. The country has implemented legislation to address these issues.

There is resistance to Turkey joining the EU. Some Turks are sceptical because they think there is a power group within the EU that wants to preserve its "white, Christian identity." Supporters of Turkey's membership argue that it is a key regional power with a large economy and the second-largest military force of NATO.

shares a part of its border, although ties are strained by Armenia's allegations that Turkey refuses to take responsibility for the Armenian genocide.

The Kars-T'bilisi Railway project is a major joint investment project between Turkey and Georgia. Turkey is Georgia's main trading partner and second to the United States in total investment in Georgia. The railway was due to be completed in 2013. However, due to complexity of the work, the project is expected to be completed in 2014. Perhaps the most important link that the AK government is pursuing is with the EU.

UNEMPLOYMENT

Although Turkey has natural resources that could ensure its material prosperity, the unstable economic climate since 2000 has affected many Turks. A high birthrate and the migration of the unemployed to the urban areas in search of work contribute to the problem. The cities cannot accommodate the numbers that pour in each year from the countryside. The peasants settle on the fringes of Istanbul and Ankara in shoddily built homes called *gecekondu* (GEDJ-erh KOHN-doo), which means built overnight. An Ottoman tradition says that if a house can be built in one night, the builders have a right to live there. A large number of Ankara's and Istanbul's residents live in *gecekondu* areas. The population density in Istanbul is 21 times higher than the population density of Turkey.

With overcrowding and unemployment rampant in the cities, vast numbers of unemployed Turks have gone to European countries to work. Germany is traditionally the first choice for migrant workers, but Belgium, Switzerland, and Sweden are also popular. In 2012, about 1.2 million Turks were working abroad.

MIGRATION TO EUROPE

Although workers have to make social and cultural adjustments when living in a new country, Turkish communities have developed in many European capitals, and migrants going there know they will not be alone. In recent years, however, the practice of migrating to Europe for work has suffered a setback for two reasons.

First, the economic downturn has depressed the European economies, and Turkish workers now find themselves competing for work with the native unemployed. Second, the enlargement of the EU to include a number of eastern European countries has decreased the demand for Turkish workers.

A woman weaves a *kilim* carpet in Cappadocia. These pieces will eventually find their way into a local shop or be exported.

HANDICRAFTS

Turkey's handicrafts are more than works of art; they are also sources of revenue. Tourists are attracted to *kilim* (KEE-lim), colorful pileless rugs woven on looms in bold patterns. The high-quality carpets are made with natural dyes. Traditionally, carpets were an essential gift for newlyweds to start their own homes.

Copperware is no longer as common as it was when, along with a carpet, it was given as a wedding present. Copperware used to be purely handmade, but today the majority of copper products found in the bazaars are manufactured. Nevertheless, there is a long tradition in copper design work, and many handmade pieces in traditional shapes are still being sold.

Leatherwork is another craft that has been practiced for centuries in Turkey. The skin of young animals is used for high-quality items because it is soft. There are large workshops in Istanbul that cater to the domestic and tourist markets.

Meerschaum is a white, absorbent clay quarried in the west of Anatolia. Turkey is the only country that possesses sufficient reserves to make it commercially viable to excavate. It is fashioned into pipes, cigarette holders, and decorative items. The government is encouraging the preservation of traditional crafts at state-supported craft guilds and shops.

FARMING

Turkey has been self-sufficient in food production since the 1980s. Agriculture provides jobs for 25 percent of the population, and together with fishing and forestry, it accounts for 9.3 percent of the gross domestic product (GDP). The country's large agricultural sector accounts for 25.5 percent of employment. Turkey is the world's largest producer of hazelnut, cherry, fig, apricot, quince, and pomegranate. The tobacco industry is principally located on the Black Sea coast, and the domestic market is just as important as the export market.

Meerschaum pipes sold at the Grand Bazaar of Istanbul.

Vineyards and orchards cover around 10,000 square miles (26,000 square km), providing valuable yields of wine, citrus fruit, and olives. The Black Sea coast is especially well-known for its high concentration of small family estates that derive their income from hazelnuts; tea is grown in the northeast of the country, where there is more rainfall. Both crops are also exported.

Farmers in Turkey face the problem of fragmented holdings. This means that farms generally consist of many small lots often separated from one another by considerable distances, making it difficult for farmers to have a piece of land big enough to plant crops over one sizable area. Eighty-five percent of agricultural holdings are under 24.7 acres (10 hectares).

Potato pickers in Cappadocia. Although Turkey is industrializing rapidly, agriculture is important to the Turkish economy.

INDUSTRY

Turkey's economic base is now so broad it does not rely solely on any one industry to power its economy. Industry and services have long eclipsed agriculture as the backbone of the Turkish economy.

AUTOMOBILE In 2011 Turkey's total vehicle production (excluding tractors) was around 1,189,131, while in 2010 it was the largest commercial vehicle producer in Europe. However, production declined to 1,072,339 in 2012 due to a shrinking export market.

The automotive industry is an important part of the economy since the late 1960s. The companies that operate in the sector are mainly located in the Marmara Region. With a cluster of carmakers and parts suppliers, the Turkish automotive sector has become an integral part of the global network of production bases.

Turkey ranks tenth in the list of countries by steel production. In 2010, total steel production was 29.1 million tons.

ELECTRONICS Turkey's Vestel is currently the largest TV producer in Europe. By January 2005, Vestel and its rival Turkish electronics and whiteware brand Beko accounted for more than half of all TV sets manufactured in Europe. The EU market share of Turkish companies in consumer electronics has increased significantly following the Customs Union agreement signed between the EU and Turkey, especially in color TVs from 5 percent in 1995 to more than 50 percent in 2012.

CONSTRUCTION In 2009 the Turkish construction industry was the second-largest in the world, losing out only to China. One of the world's largest development projects is the Southeastern Anatolia Project (GAP); the project involves the construction of dams and hydroelectric power plants on the Tigris and Euphrates rivers, including 22 dams, 19 hydraulic power plants, and the irrigation of 4.4 million acres (1.7 million hectares) of land. Upon the completion of this undertaking, it was planned that per capita income will rise by 209 percent and about 3.8 million people will be provided with jobs.

TOURISM Tourism also plays an important role in the national economy. The coastal areas attract sunseekers, while inland the amazing number of historic sites draws travellers from around the world. In 2012, the number of visitors rose to 36,776,645, who contributed over $23 billion to Turkey's revenues. Over the years, Turkey has emerged as a popular tourist destination for many Europeans, competing with Greece, Italy, and Spain.

Tourists bathing in the Antique Pool of Hierapolis, one of Turkey's many UNESCO sites. Tourism is a major source of revenue for the country.

Turkey is one of the world's leading shipbuilding nations. In 2010 Turkish shipyards ranked sixth in the world in terms of the number of ordered ships, and also fourth in the world in terms of the number of ordered mega yachts in 2012.

INTERNET LINKS

www.enjoyturkey.com/info/facts/Economy.htm
Interesting facts about Turkey's economy.

www.europeanunionplatform.org/
A number of articles which highlight Turkey's tumultuous relationship with the European Union.

http://ec.europa.eu/trade/creating-opportunities/bilateral-relations/countries/turkey/
Turkey's Trade Statistics with the EU.

ENVIRONMENT

Lake Van is home to the Church of the Holy Cross, a 10th century Armenian church located on Akdamar island.

5

ONE OF TURKEY'S GREATEST challenges in the 21st century is to preserve its natural environment while taking advantage of opportunities offered by technological developments to further build the economy. Both objectives have long-term implications, but the latter often commands greater support, giving rise to several major environmental issues.

One such issue surrounds the building of dams and hydroelectric power plants. Dams disrupt the flow of rivers, which are the natural habitat for diverse species of fish and other aquatic life.

Environmentalists are also alarmed at the high volume of traffic passing through the Bosporus Strait. Massive oil tankers make up the bulk of the traffic, and an accident could result in an oil spill with disastrous consequences to human and animal life, as well as to historic sites along the Turkish coast.

TURKEY'S FLORA AND FAUNA

Turkey's natural environment is home to a varied flora. Large areas of western and southern Turkey are covered by Mediterranean-type vegetation consisting of thick underbrush in the lowlands and deciduous and coniferous forests in the highlands. Along the northern margins is the densely wooded region of the country, while the eastern Black Sea coast is covered by subtropical forest.

One of the crucial factors that would contribute towards environmental protection is the increase in awareness and participation of the people. Sadly, only a small minority of Turks believe environmental issues are a major concern, despite Turkey's beautiful natural environment.

The country's Mediterranean climate allows plants characteristic of Europe to flourish. The dry and arid terrain of central Anatolia is suitable for plants that normally grow near the seashore because a high evaporation rate brings salt to the surface of the soil.

Turkey boasts a richer fauna than any other country in Europe. Deer, foxes, wolves, boars, beavers, hyenas, and bears inhabit the country's varied habitats. Partridges, quail, and bustards are common game birds.

ENDANGERED ANIMALS Turkey's Aegean and Mediterranean shores provide a refuge for monk seals and loggerhead turtles, while its wetlands house colonies of numerous endangered species, such as the Dalmatian pelican, pygmy cormorant, and the slender billed curlew, as well as flamingos, wild ducks, and geese. Under the auspices of the Ministry of the Environment a program is underway to protect the last surviving colonies of monk seal along Turkey's Mediterranean and Aegean coasts. The fact that the species has survived along Turkey's shores is due to the preservation of the natural environment in many areas and low-pollution levels.

LAKE VAN

Lake Van is the largest body of water in Turkey. It is located in eastern Anatolia near Turkey's border with Iran. Measuring 74 miles (119 km) wide and covering an area of 1,434 square miles (3,714 square km), the lake fills a low-lying basin surrounded by plains, mountains, and volcanoes. The lake derives its name from the ancient capital of the Urartian civilization that was located on the eastern shore of the lake between 10 and 8 B.C.

Lake Van has no outlet. Centuries ago, the lava flow from a volcanic eruption blocked the lake's link to the Murat River. Today, the lake is an enclosed basin of salty, brackish water fed by rainfall and melting snow from the surrounding mountains. The hot, eastern Anatolian climate causes a high rate of evaporation, resulting in the lake's high salinity. As a result, no fish can survive in the lake's salty water except for the *darekh* (duh-REH-keh), a freshwater fish that has adapted to the lake's water. The *darekh* is a type of herring.

A supervised breeding colony of the eastern bald ibis (*Geronticus eremite*), on the verge of world extinction, is alive and well at Birecik in the southeast of Anatolia.

Near the town of Silifke where the Göksu River flows into the eastern Mediterranean is a delta area that has become a protected bird reservation. More than 300 bird species reside in the delta, and millions of migratory birds are attracted to the two large lagoons and the long sand spit that enclose the water. Rare species of birds spotted at the delta include kingfishers and the purple Swamp-hen, which breeds only in the Göksu Delta. The lagoons are busiest with bird life during the nesting periods in spring and in the fall, when flocks gather before departing for Africa to spend winter. The delta is also a nesting ground for Loggerhead and Green turtles, as well as the Blue crab.

The Göksu Delta is one of the best preserved wetlands in the world. It is recognized under the Ramsar Convention as a wetland of international importance. Turkey has five such wetlands.

The lake region is the original habitat of the Turkish Van cat. White in color and distinguished by its different colored eyes—one eye is golden yellow and the other is blue—the cat is said to be able to swim in the lake. Another creature said to inhabit the lake is of a more dubious origin. The Lake Van monster was first sighted in 1995. Witnesses have reported seeing a long and dark creature, which looks like a dinosaur, swimming in the lake. Skeptics have dismissed the claims, suggesting that it is a hoax to attract tourists to the region.

The lake is also a resting stop for a variety of birds migrating to Africa each year. The most regular visitors are flamingos, cormorants, pelicans, and gulls.

THE GAP

The Southeastern Anatolia Project, known as the GAP, is a large-scale engineering project aimed at generating hydroelectric power and irrigating the dry land of southeastern Anatolia. Initiated in 1976, it is one of the largest of its kind. The project involves building 22 dams and 19 hydroelectric plants on the Tigris and Euphrates rivers. The plants, when completed, will have the capacity to provide 22 percent of the country's electric power. The GAP

Although Lake Van is situated at an altitude of 5,380 feet (1,639 m) with harsh winters, it does not freeze due to its high salinity except occasionally the shallow northern section.

The Birecik Dam over the Euphrates river is one of the 21 dams of the Southeastern Anatolia Project of Turkey.

The Atatürk dam, completed in 1990, is the fifth-largest dam in the world and the largest in Turkey. Twenty-two dams and 19 hydroelectric power plants have been built under the GAP

will also be able to irrigate 1.82 million hectares (17 million square meters) of land previously blighted by a lack of water.

The GAP's objectives are to expand agricultural land and provide electricity for towns and cities in the region to support further economic development. Gradual improvements in infrastructure, forestry, education, and health care will yield self-sufficient communities for generations. However, environmentalists are concerned about the GAP's negative impact on the environment.

The GAP has come under severe criticism not only from environmentalists, but also from human rights groups and neighbors Syria and Iraq. The source of water for the GAP is the Euphrates-Tigris basin, and both the Euphrates and the Tigris are major rivers that flow downstream to Syria and Iraq. Because of this, GAP is one of the world's most well protected dam projects, especially against aircraft. GAP also almost came to a complete halt in the early 1990s due to the high level of Kurdish terrorist (PKK) activities in the region. The PKK is not only blamed for a number of funding cuts as funds were diverted to support the counterterrorism effort, but is also blamed for damaging several dams and canals, as well as killing engineers working at the dams.

The Birecik dam, operational since 2000, has drawn protest from archaeologists and historians, who claim that it has caused damage to the region's rich archaeological heritage. Several cultural sites have been submerged, including a royal tomb and a mosque built by a sultan. The area was also home to the 2,000-year-old Roman settlement of Zeugma. On June 2005, the second-largest mosaic museum in the world was opened in Gaziantep displaying 35 pieces of unearthed mosaics and a Mars statue from Zeugma. The GAP project extends over nine administrative regions. Three dams have been built over the Euphrates: Karakaya, Atatürk, and Birecik. Seven airports have been finished and active. The GAP cargo airport in Şırnak, which is also the biggest in Turkey, has been completed.

STRAITS ACCIDENTS

Between 1953 and 2002, 461 serious accidents have taken place in the Turkish straits. In 1979, a Greek tanker collided with the Romanian Independenta *tanker. The* Independenta *exploded, killing 43 people and spilling 94,000 tons of its oil cargo into the Bosporus. The resulting fire lasted for weeks.*

With a history of tanker accidents and the risk of such accidents occurring in the future, the Turkish government initiated the Traffic Separation System in 1998. This allows Turkey to control the number of ships using the straits at any time based on the size of the ship. This system ensures that large ships will have enough space to navigate through the straits and minimizes the risk of a collision with another large tanker.

OIL SPILLS

The Bosporus is one of the world's busiest shipping routes. Each year, an estimated 55,000 ships, of which 10,000 are tankers carrying tons of oil or natural gas, pass through the narrow Bosporus waterway that connects the oil-rich Black Sea region to the Mediterranean. With the volume of tanker traffic going through this slim, winding passage—there are 12 abrupt turns— the Turkish government and environmentalists are in agreement that there is a high risk of a maritime disaster with calamitous consequences. The country has had shipping accidents in the past: from colliding tankers to ships running aground or into coastal buildings.

Istanbul, a UNESCO World Heritage City with 13,256 million inhabitants, lies alongside this dangerous waterway. Turkey's coast is also lined with historic archeological sites. A major oil spill will badly affect Turkey's cultural heritage, natural environment, and the lives of people living by the coast.

Aware of the potential for widescale disaster, the Turkish government has tried to control the number of oil tankers passing through the Bosporus. However, Turkey's power is limited, since the Bosporus is an international waterway. In 2003 a $45 million radar monitoring system was installed on Bosporus and Dardanelles Straits to help ships navigate through the waterway. The Baku—Tbilisi—Ceyhan pipeline was completed on 28 May 2006.

DEFORESTATION

Anatolia was once blanketed in forests, and tree-cutting was confined to local people seeking fuel and clearing land for farming. The 20th century, however, has seen deforestation on a large scale. Half of Turkey's forests have been destroyed by forest fires, some of which were started deliberately to clear large areas of land for development. Today, the Turkish government has embarked on reforestation and conservation programs in some areas. Forests, however, are still being cleared to make way for dams.

Some 27.2 percent of Turkey's surface area is covered by forests, and approximately 50 percent of these forests are already degraded. In addition to afforestation, erosion control and range improvement measures, the National Mobilization and Erosion Control Act was put into force in 1995. The main objective of the act is to ensure participation and contribution of all related governmental and nongovernmental organizations, private sector and local people, and to provide additional financial resources for combating deforestation and erosion control activities at a national level.

The Ministry of Forestry has started to encourage the private sector and farmers to establish private plantations by means of new and innovative regulations. In addition, the Law on Development of Forest Villagers has entered into force, and the interest rates of the credits given to support forest villagers have been reduced.

Other measures taken to combat deforestation include tree breeding activities, establishment of germ-plasma banks, and in-situ and ex-situ conservation programs.

Unique and threatened forest ecosystems and the forests located within high-sloped areas are not subject to forest production. These kind of areas are classified as protected forests or protected areas. Regeneration by using clear cutting methods in large forest areas has not been implemented since 1992.

Issues which have been addressed only in part so far are the following: development of public education in forestry, identification of research and information exchange linkages, using indigenous knowledge, remote sensing, environmental impact assessment, carrying out investment analysis and feasibility studies, promotion of small-scale forest-based industries, assessment of forest industry efficiency, and promotion of ecotourism.

Turkey supports the development of a legally binding instrument on management, conservation, and sustainable development of all types of forests. The First Forestry Assembly was held in 1993. The decisions taken by the Assembly were being considered all important forestry activities expressed by the UNCED at Rio, 1992. In 1997, the XI World Forestry Congress was held in Turkey.

RECYCLING IN TURKEY

There is conservation going on in Turkey, but not as defined by the West per se. For instance, most food is made from scratch and none is wasted. Leftovers are kept for the next meal. The Turks are careful with what power and water they use because the cost of electricity and water is high. Solar power in Turkey is used for heating water given the large amount of sunlight Turkey has. The solar panels quickly recover the cost of the installation given the savings in electricity. They also make use of thermal heat from the ground which in some towns like Dikili is used to heat most of the homes and provide hot water.

What is thrown away in the bins is minimal and what can be salvaged is taken by the rag-and-bone man. The rag-and-bone men then take the scrap and the waste plastic and paper to collection points and are paid for what they bring. This waste is then taken and recycled, but it is not seen as recycling but a job and a way of life in Turkey.

GREEK SHIPS The crisis-hit Greek maritime sector is sending its ships to Turkey for recycling. Some 85 percent of the ships sent to AliaĐa in the Aegean province of Đzmir for recycling so far this year came from Greece. In 2011, 341 ships from Greece were sent to Turkey for recycling, while the figure was 67 in the first quarter of 2012.

BATTERY RECYCLING Nearly 9,000 tons of batteries are annually sold on the market in Turkey, whereas only 325 tons are collected for recycling and disposal, revealing the hazard they pose to the environment, especially due to the mercury and lead batteries contain.

TURTLES AT RISK

Near the tourist town of Dalyan is the beautiful Iztuzu beach, one of the last nesting sites of the Loggerhead turtle (Caretta caretta) in the Mediterranean. The turtles lay their eggs in the sand at a number of sites along this stretch of Turkey's western Mediterranean coastline. The beach came to attention in the late 1980s when developers wanted to build a luxury hotel on it. Conservationists succeeded in their opposition, and the nesting sites are now protected.

Two species of turtles breed in Turkey, where efforts to protect them have been extremely successful. A tourism development project at Köycegiz has also been scrapped to preserve the breeding grounds of Caretta caretta, and the lake and marshes of Köycegiz have now been declared a Specially Protected Area. These measures were received with a standing ovation by the Standing Committee of Bern Convention of the Council of Europe in 1989, and cited as an example for other countries to follow. Studies of the turtles along all Turkey's shores have been launched, and seventeen sand beaches of foremost importance as breeding grounds for turtles are kept under constant observation by the Turtle Preservation Committee.

There are no battery recycling facilities in Turkey and so rechargeable ones, which make up to 15 percent of collected batteries, are being sent to some European countries.

NATIONAL PARKS AND RESERVES IN TURKEY

As of 2008, there were 39 National Parks all around Turkey, and their total surface reached 2,169,011 acres (877,771 hectares).

OLYMPOS BEYDAGLARI NATIONAL PARK This gorgeous park consists of the Mt. Olympos, an extension of the regionally dominant Bey-Daglari mountain range, and the Saricinar Dag mountain. The park is bordered by the sea to the east and south with a coastline formed by precipitous cliffs or long, narrow sandy beaches below the Bogaz plateau. Vegetation is markedly altitudinal, rising from coastal maquis and pine woods to montane cedar forest and alpine steppe.

KÖPRÜLÜ CANYON NATIONAL PARK Köprülü Canyon is a canyon and a National Park in the Province of Antalya, Turkey. Covering an area of 36,614 hectares (366 square km), it was established as a national park by the Ministry of Forest on December 12, 1973. The canyon is 1,300 feet (396 m) deep in some places and stretches for 8.7 miles (14 km) along the Köprü River. The Roman Oluklu Bridge over the canyon and the Bugrum Bridge over the Kocadere stream were considered engineering feats of their time.

YEDIGOLLER NATIONAL PARK The Yeniçağa crossing on the Ankara-Istanbul highway leads to Yedigöller National Park. The Yedigöller consists of seven small lakes, teeming with trout, fed by the same sparkling mountain stream. The first cultured trout farm in Turkey was set up here in 1969 and this area is popular with fishermen. Beech, oaks, hornbeams, alders, black pine, Scotch pine, firs, elm, and lime trees grow here. This is also a deer protection area.

The Köprülü Kanyon River in Antalya.

INTERNET LINKS

www.mymerhaba.com/Yedi-G%C3%B6ller-Seven-Lakes-in-Turkey-969.html

Information on the Yedigoller National Park in Turkey.

www.skyscrapercity.com/showthread.php?t=165244

Stunning photos of Seven Lakes National Park in Bolu, Turkey.

www.allaboutturkey.com/millipark.htm

A listing of all the National Parks of Turkey, together with details of the various Turkish pieces of legislation to protect the environment.

THE TURKS

A Turkish girl in ethnic clothing at festival in Bergama. The Turks are a mixture of many ancient nationalities, including the Hittites, the Greeks, the Persians, and the Seljuk Turks.

6

TODAY, A TURK IS ANYONE who is a citizen of the Republic of Turkey. In a broad sense, Turks include people of Turkish descent, as well as people whose ancestors adopted the country as their homeland. In a stricter sense, the word Turk is an ethnic label that refers to a descendant of the early Turks.

The early Turks came from Central Asia into Anatolia. They shared the land with Greeks, Armenians, Arabs, and Kurds. During Ottoman rule, Turkish territory increased, and Turks established themselves beyond Anatolia. As the empire collapsed, these Turks returned to Anatolia. At the same time, people from the Caucasus sought refuge in Anatolia when the Russians invaded their homeland. These peoples, such as the Laz, were not of Turkish descent but were accepted into Turkish society.

Between World War I and the formation of the Republic of Turkey in 1923, many ethnic minorities fled the country. Today, the Kurds are the only significant ethnic minority left and account for 18 percent of the national population.

THE TURKS

The Turks have a mixed heritage. Long before Turkish-speaking people arrived, the land that is now Turkey was home to many other races and tribes. The Hittites created the first important empire in the area. Later came the Greeks, Persians, and Romans. The Celts and the Jews were there just before the Christian era. In the east and southeast, Kurds

Contrary to nationalist dogma, studies of population genetics have indicated that the modern Anatolian Turks are genetically influenced by indigenous (pre-Islamic) Anatolian populations.

Students on their way to school in Istanbul. All Turkish children, especially boys, are the pride and joy of their parents.

In addition, due to migration, a large Turkish diaspora has been established, particularly in Europe. There are also large Turkish communities living in Australia, the Middle East, North America, and the former Soviet Union.

and Armenians were prominent. When the Turks finally arrived, they did not expel these peoples but assimilated them instead. The result is that today's Turks are a genetic mix of European and Asian. Some Turks are olive-skinned with black hair and brown eyes. Others are blond and blue-eyed with fair skin.

The original homeland of the Turks was in Central and Eastern Asia, around what is now Mongolia. The earliest written evidence of their language dates back to the eighth century. Over centuries, the Turks moved continually westward in search of arable land and food. By the 12th century, they had occupied Anatolia. For centuries, the Ottoman Empire was the enemy of Christendom, and Europe viewed the empire and its actions negatively. The word Turk soon came to describe anyone whose behavior was unkind or even savage. Turks had a reputation for violence, but today, Turks are perceived as friendly and hospitable.

The contemporary citizens of Turkey have a sense of national pride that can be attributed to the reforms of Atatürk. Atatürk urged the Turks to take pride in their new country, which emerged after the chaos surrounding the break up of the Ottoman Empire. A proud, nationalistic spirit is still part of the Turkish mentality.

THE LAZ

There are two main groups of Laz in Turkey. The first group lives in the eastern half of the Black Sea region, in Rize and Artvin provinces. The second group are the descendants of immigrants who escaped the war between the Ottoman and Russian Empires in the late 19th century and settled in Adapazarı, Sapanca, Yalova, and Bursa, in western and eastern parts of the Black Sea and Marmara regions, respectively.

Turks loosely refer to anyone living in the eastern part of Turkey's Black Sea region as Laz. The Laz people are a small ethnic group in a particular section of the eastern coast beyond the city of Trabzon and in certain inland localities. The Laz came from Georgia, their homeland for centuries. Under the influence of the Byzantine Empire, the Laz were Christianized. Under the Ottomans, they converted to Islam. For some time the Laz kept their Christian names even though they had taken Islamic names. They even practiced both religions and came to be known as crypto-Christians. Today, the Laz are nearly all Muslim and are fully integrated into the Turkish way of life. They continue to speak Lazi, a Caucasian language similar to Georgian. The main Laz towns are Pazar, Ardesen, and Hopa.

Turkish women and child in Rize. Their Caucasian looks point to their European ancestry.

Laz men are distinguished from Turks by their red hair and sharper features. Their success in business, especially in the shipping industry, has enabled them to lead a comfortable life. Their expertise in shipping has a long history, going back to the days when they were famous as pirates and skilled boat builders. Today, traditional Laz dress is rarely seen as most Laz wear Western-style clothing.

The Laz live by the coast, with the Pontic Mountains behind them. Many small rivers flow down to the sea, and the Laz use the surrounding trees to build small bridges, chalets, and *seranders* (serh-AN-derhs), which are small buildings erected on stilts to store corn used for making the region's distinctive bread. The Laz region was once home to a large Greek community, but most of its members were deported after World War I. Today, it is rare to hear Greek being spoken in and around the region.

It is estimated there are 250,000 Laz in Turkey, and 30,000 native speakers of Laz in Turkey.

The Kurdish people do not have their own country. They number about 20 million to 25 million and can be found living in Turkey, Iraq, Iran, Russia, Syria, Germany, Armenia, Georgia, Kazakhstan, Lebanon, Syria, and Eastern Europe. About half of the global Kurdish population live in Turkey. If the Kurds were ever to establish their own homeland, Kurdistan, it would occupy a mountainous area divided between Turkey, Iran, and Iraq. Kurdistan means Land of the Kurds. Claims for Kurdish autonomy have their basis in a treaty signed in 1920 that promised Kurds an independent Kurdistan after the dissolution of the Ottoman Empire. The treaty was renegotiated and the Kurds became stateless.

The Kurds rose in rebellion against the former government of Iraq. In 1988 thousands of Kurdish refugees fled to Turkey to escape chemical warfare attacks by the Iraqi government. In 1990—91 following the defeat of Iraq in the Gulf Wars, it seemed as if they might be successful in achieving autonomy, but this has not happened.

The Gulf War in 2003 triggered alarm in Turkey. Since 1999 the Kurds in northern Iraq had achieved some autonomy. The Turkish government feared that the Iraqi Kurds might extend their area of control and inspire Kurds in Turkey to seek their own independence.

THE HAMSHEN

The Hamshen inhabit the eastern Black Sea provinces of Rize and Artvin. They are believed to have descended from the early Armenians, who immigrated to the Black Sea region in A.D. 790. In the 8th century, the Armenian princes Hamam and Shapuh Amatuni lost their domains in Artaz to the Arabs and moved to the Byzantine Empire with 12,000 of their people. During the Byzantine age, many of them became Christians. Under Ottoman rule, they converted to Islam. The Hamshen remain ethnically distinct today because of their geographical isolation. Muslim Hamshen can also be found today in the towns of Hopa and Rize.

The Hamshen, like the Laz, have Caucasian looks that separate them from mainstream Turks. Many of the easternmost Hemshinli villages in Turkey preserve their original Armenian dialects, commonly referred to as *Homshetsma* or HemÐince by their speakers. They are known for their culinary skills especially in making pastries and puddings. Many of the prestigious pastry shops in Istanbul and Ankara are owned by Hamshen.

Hamshen women still wear some of their traditional clothing, especially the brightly patterned handwoven scarves often worn as turbans. The scarf material, however, is not woven in Turkey but in India. This may be a throwback to Byzantine days, when nearby Trabzon prospered as a bustling commercial center on the Silk Road.

Like the Laz, the Hamshen have access to the forests of oak, beech, birch, maple, and chestnut. They use the wood of these trees to complete the top half of their *yayla* (YAI-lah), which are their traditional dwellings built of stone to half their height and then completed in timber. Constructed in the uplands, most of them are uninhabitable until spring because of the harsh winter.

INTERNET LINKS

www.turkishodyssey.com/turkey/culture/people.htm
All about the Turkish people and their customs.

www.hemshin.org/about_us.html
The webpage strives to raise awareness about Hamshen people.

http://worldpress.org/Europe/3790.cfm
Illuminating article about the Kurds struggle for identity in Turkey.

The movie *Momi (Grandma)* was filmed in the Hamshen dialect in 2000. Directed by Ozcan Alper, it was the first motion picture in the Homshetsi language (Hemsince or Armenian).

LIFESTYLE

Shoppers at the Demiroren shopping centre on Istiklal Cadess in Istanbul. In more strict Islamic cultures, only the men do the shopping.

7

TURKEY IS A LARGE COUNTRY with a diverse population. Although nearly all Turks adhere to the same religious practices, significant differences in lifestyle do exist. The fundamental difference is evident between life in the countryside and life in the urban areas where 70 percent of the Turkish population now lives.

There are also important social differences between Turkish women and men. But despite these differences, there are also many traits that all Turks have in common.

NATIONAL PRIDE

Turks are an immensely proud people, not in an arrogant manner or a flag-waving style, but in a more personal way. Atatürk is often credited with having created this sense of national identity, although to some extent he merely cultivated feelings that were already there.

A famous remark of Atatürk's serves as a clue to the kind of nationalism experienced by many Turks. He said: "So what does it matter if our regime does not resemble democracy, does not resemble socialism, does not resemble anything? Gentlemen, we should be proud of not resembling anything; because we resemble ourselves!"

This last remark, "Biz bize benzeriz" (we resemble ourselves), may seem to be an obvious truth, but it also indicates a belief in one's own distinct, and therefore special, identity. It has been said that a Turk's first duty is to be proud.

The Turkish urban lifestyle is comparable to that of any Western country, with all modern amenities available at a much lower cost than in the EU, which Turkey keeps hoping to join.

THE POSITION OF WOMEN

A female university student. Modesty and conservatism still prevail among the modern women in Turkey.

The right to vote for women was granted nationwide in Turkey in 1934. Theoretically, Turkish women were far ahead of many of their western sisters at that time, for instance in France where women only gained the right to vote in 1944.

Kemal Atatürk took on a great challenge when he set out to modernize and secularize a society that was, and still is, very patriarchal. Atatürk gave women access to higher education and better paying jobs by opening high schools, colleges, and the civil service to women. He fixed a minimum age for marriage, and introduced the right of women to divorce and retain custody of their children. He also gave women the right to testify in court.

Under Islamic law, although women could testify, the testimony of one man was equal to that of two women.

Although Atatürk's reforming spirit is still at work, the fundamental position of women has not improved. For generations, women have been raised and taught to be submissive to male authority, not just their father or husband, but brothers, younger and older, and male in-laws. Despite modern laws that proclaim the equality of the sexes, male superiority remains an unquestionable part of daily life. In rural parts of the country, women are rarely seen out alone in public places such as restaurants or beaches, but in the bigger cities, women are becoming more liberal.

A great boost for women's rights came in 1993 with the election of Turkey's first female prime minister, Tansu Ciller. Ciller is also the first woman to lead an Islamic country and has helped introduce legislation to aid women's rights.

In 2001, the country's Grand National Assembly approved changes to the Turkish civil code that gave women the same rights as the country's male citizens. The code has remained relatively unaltered since 1926, and this is seen as a huge step for Turkey in aligning itself with EU standards. Legislation now allows married women to work without their husbands' permission and to choose a profession they like. Women can keep their maiden names and be recognized as the legal head of a household. Women and men also have equal say in the family on issues such as where to live. A new law came into effect in 2003 whereby a couple's wealth is to be distributed equally between them in the event of a divorce.

CHILDBIRTH

Such is the position of women that, among the more traditionally-minded, the birth of a son is far more important than the birth of a daughter. In some cases, magical prescriptions and superstitions are used in order to ensure the birth of a male child.

Immediately after the birth of a child, and for the 40 days that follow, tradition dictates that the child should be protected because it is very vulnerable to the malign influence of witches and devils. One way of trying to protect the newborn is by "salting." Salting is a custom in which the baby's body is rubbed all over with salt in the belief that this will give the child strength to resist harmful influences. Another practice, no longer as common as it once was, involves the placing of a tortoise under the child's pillow at night. It is believed that the tortoise will protect the infant.

Concern for a newborn is related to a more fundamental fear of the *nazar* (na-ZAR), or evil eye. Directly translated, it means "the look." Traditionally, infants are deliberately dressed in as unflattering a way as possible for the first 40 days of their lives. For example, the baby's clothes might be put on backward to try to deceive the *nazar*.

As children grow up, the need for protection against evil forces continues. When relatives and friends praise a young child, they will often add the word *maashallah* (MAH-SHAH-ahl-lah), which is an invocation to God for security. Turkish children sometimes wear a blue bead as a talisman or charm for protection, especially against the blue-eyed, who are believed to be able to impart harm through an evil look.

CIRCUMCISION

Every Turkish male, if he is a Muslim, will be circumcised between the ages of two and 14. If the child is older, the act of circumcision may become part of an initiation ceremony that marks the change of status from childhood to adulthood. It is common for younger boys to be circumcised at the same time as their older brothers.

A boy is dressed in a traditional costume for his Circumcision Ceremony. For Turkish males circumcision is an important event in their lives. The fortitude shown by the boys enhances the family's reputation.

Forty-three percent of the working population of Turkey are women.

Among educated, middle-class families in the cities, it is becoming increasingly more common for the circumcision to take place in a local private clinic or hospital. Traditionally, the event is cause for rejoicing, and a celebration party is organized to mark the occasion. In rural communities, the cost of such parties is often shared among family members and relatives who consider it an act of piety to contribute to the expenses.

The act of circumcision itself is traditionally accompanied by its own rituals. When the doctor performs the circumcision, male friends and relatives clap, and a pistol is sometimes fired in celebration.

Turkish men enjoying themselves at a teahouse in Istanbul. In Turkish society, male friends greet each other with affection.

A MALE WORLD

Turkish men are very demonstrative of their affection for one another. It is not uncommon in Turkey to see two men walking down the street holding hands. When men meet, they often embrace and kiss in a more carefree and affectionate way than many women do.

Turkish men often socialize exclusively among themselves. The coffeehouse or small village eatery is the traditional meeting place for men of all ages. Women do not generally frequent such places, and usually the waiters and managers are men.

A characteristic trait of the Turkish male is *namus* (NAH-moose), which means honor. An insult directed at one's personal or family honor is taken very seriously and sometimes results in violence.

The notion of honor is closely related to that of family loyalty. An individual's sense of grievance over an insult can develop over time into a bloody feud between members of rival families. Such feuds can last for generations and periodically develop into serious acts of violence and death. Even today, newspaper reports tell of murders, known as honor killings, resulting from arguments between men over matters of their family's honor and loyalty.

"He's a lucky man who can say, 'I am a Turk.'"
—Kemal Atatürk

FAMILY LIFE

The family is at the heart of Turkish life. The most common form of celebration among family members is over a meal.

In rural areas households remain large because the extended family lives together under one roof. A family consisting of more than seven members is not uncommon. There is an unspoken agreement that older members of a family need to be supported after their retirement, and it is common for the parents to live with a child after they grow old. In extended families, respect is accorded first to the oldest male. An aged grandfather will continue to be treated as the highest authority on all subjects even if all the daily decisions are made by the younger generation. A middle-aged man will still rise to his feet when his father enters a room.

The importance of family life is probably best demonstrated during *Seker Bayrami*, a celebration that marks the end of the religious month of fasting. On this day, formal visits are made to the eldest member of the family, whose hand is ceremoniously kissed as a mark of respect.

A bride is accompanied by her entourage in a traditional wedding ceremony in Tercan. A Turkish wedding is usually accompanied by music and dancing. A modern white wedding gown may be worn by brides in towns or cities.

WEDDINGS

Traditional ceremonial wedding rituals are becoming less common in cities and towns. Today, an urban wedding in Turkey usually consists of a short, simple exchange of the marriage vows in the city hall. This is usually followed by a private reception, where food and drink are consumed and traditional music is played.

In the countryside, a marriage is often a far more prolonged affair. Before a marriage is approved, a variety of matters are discussed and debated over a long period of time. The parents of both parties meet to determine the suitability of the match. The traditional practice of giving a dowry has not completely died out, although it is very rare these days.

In 1926, a minimum age for marriage was fixed at 15 for girls and 17 for boys.

After the marriage is approved, the ceremony can be planned. This often takes months. Traditionally, the ceremony includes the participation of an entire village. On her wedding day, the bride is raised on the shoulders of the villagers and brought to the bridegroom's house accompanied by a huge procession of people. Musicians follow the procession playing a medley of festive tunes.

The reception that follows is usually a noisy affair, with dancing and music that can last through the night. A wedding in the countryside is one of the few occasions when traditional folk dancing is still performed. Communal dancing is also popular at weddings. Men and women form two different lines and hold hands. The communal dance is accompanied by folk music played on traditional Turkish instruments.

A *gecekondu* in Istanbul. Badly over-crowded, Istanbul is one of the biggest cities in Europe and is continuing to grow annually largely because of migration from the countryside.

FUNERALS

In Turkey, the passing of a life is marked in a quiet, simple, and dignified manner. Funerals are traditionally attended only by men, a practice common throughout the Muslim world. The ceremony generally includes the recitation of a *mevlud* (mev-LOOD), which is a poem that celebrates the birth of the Prophet Muhammad and praises the will of Allah (God). This simplicity is carried over to the cemeteries. The dead are buried quickly, often on the day of death. Plain tombstones mark the head and foot of the grave. Tombstones, however, can be elaborate, especially for the resting place of a revered holy man. The graves of such men are sometimes treated as places of worship, and people pray at them when they are making special requests to Allah.

In small towns and rural areas, families send people to the houses of their relatives and friends to announce a death in the family and to invite them to the funeral service. In urban areas, deaths are announced through the city newspapers.

URBAN LIFE

For the educated elite, life in Istanbul or Ankara is as cosmopolitan as in other major European cities. English is commonly spoken, and families often have domestic servants, many of whom are village girls from the eastern part of the country.

Urban dwellers face problems of overcrowding, pollution, and housing shortages. The continuous influx of new residents from the countryside has resulted in an increasing number of shantytowns. These squatters' dwellings or *gecekondu*, which means built overnight, bear little resemblance to those found in slum areas in other parts of the world. These dwellings are built to last. Most are connected to the main electricity supply, and many have television sets and refrigerators.

A small elementary school in Milas. In the past, the majority of children attending junior high schools were boys.

Overcrowding in the cities has caused a severe strain on the public transportation system. One economical solution has been the *dolmus* (doll-MUSH). The word means stuffed, which is an accurate description of what commuter transportation becomes during rush hour. The *dolmus* is a car or minibus that travels on a set route, picking up passengers and dropping them off along the way. There are no recognized stops, so pedestrians simply hail them as they would a taxi. The fares are only slightly higher than those on the public buses, and during the rush hour they can get just as crowded.

The growth of the urban population is posing other problems for the authorities. With people from rural areas and foreigners streaming into the urban areas to find work, many cities cannot cope with the demand for housing and sanitation facilities. The Turkish government hopes to alleviate the housing shortages by building more apartments.

EDUCATION

In theory, education is free for every citizen in Turkey. In practice, there is a marked and far-reaching difference between the quality of schools in the countryside and those in the cities.

Villages provide compulsory elementary education for everyone up to the age of 14, but unlike in the cities, high school facilities are not available in every rural community. Children over the age of 12 who wish to continue with their education usually have to travel long distances in order to do so. When the school is too far away to commute each day, the student must board there. In the case of poorer families, the cost of sending a child away to school may prove to be too much, in which case the child's education effectively comes to an end.

For those who can afford it, there are private schools and colleges where English is taught intensively. Whether in urban or rural areas, middle-class families are beginning to recognize the importance of learning English as a tool for communication and business. About 95 percent of students attend public schools, but inadequacies of the public system increasingly motivates middle-class parents to seek private education.

Bazaars in Istanbul offer a wide variety of goods and products, from exquisite jewelry and carpets to every conceivable herb and spice. The Grand Bazaar consists of 65 streets lined with about 4,000 shops. It was first built under the reign of Sultan Mehmed the Conqueror.

RURAL LIFE

The difference between the lives of people in the countryside and those in the urban areas can be seen in nearly every aspect. Even the unifying bond of religion is affected by this difference.

A visitor to Istanbul or Ankara is not immediately reminded that Turkey is an Islamic country. Alcohol is readily available in restaurants and bars, and women socialize freely with men. Dress of both sexes is more modern and westernized than in other Islamic societies. In the rural areas of Anatolia, however, the presence of religion is much more apparent. Traditional beliefs, practices, and dress are still commonplace.

The majority of people in the countryside are peasants who earn their living by cultivating cash crops such as hazelnuts, tea, and sugar beets. Families are larger, and girls marry young. Polygamy is illegal according to Turkish law, but it has been a traditional feature of Turkish rural life for centuries, and it is believed that polygamy is still practiced in the remote areas of the country.

THE *BAKKAL* AND THE BAZAAR

Although supermarkets exist in Turkey, the *bakkal* (BUCK-aal) is still the place where both rural and urban shoppers go for their everyday needs. The *bakkal* is a small traditional shop that stocks basic foods and beverages. It is nearly always privately owned, and the proprietor usually works behind the counter serving the regular customers.

The bazaar, a Persian word meaning market, is found in the main towns throughout Turkey. Bazaars originated in Ottoman times, and the concept is basically the same as that behind the modern shopping mall. Various domed buildings are connected to one another by covered arcades, with different parts of the bazaar specializing in certain items. Istanbul has the most famous of all bazaars, the Grand Bazaar, said to be the largest in the world. Carpets, silver, ceramics, leather goods, pots and pans, and everything else that might be required in the home are found in the different sections. Fixed prices are not displayed, but the Turkish shopper will always know what degree of bargaining is required.

INTERNET LINKS

www.brighthubeducation.com/social-studies-help/15601-birth-and-death-traditions-in-turkey/
All about birth and death traditions in Turkey.

www.turkishculture.org/lifestyles/ceremonies-536.htm
All about getting married in Turkey and the different permutations of marriage throughout the years.

www.denverpost.com/nationworld/ci_20505217/turkey-slipping-womens-rights-groups-say
An article about worrying lapses on women's rights that have occurred in Turkey.

RELIGION

Every town in Turkey has at least one mosque, and Istanbul is especially famous for its Blue Mosque. The mosque took its name from the blue Iznik tiles of its interior. Work on the construction of this imposing building began in 1609 and took seven years to complete.

THE TURKS CONVERTED to Islam during the course of their migration to the West over a thousand years ago. Before their conversion, they were likely influenced by ancient Chinese beliefs and the worship of a sun god. Traces of this earlier system of belief can still be detected today. It is one explanation why farmers in some rural areas beat large drums and shoot off guns to mark an eclipse of the sun.

ISLAM

In Arabic, Islam means submission to the will of Allah (God). The religion originated in Arabia during the seventh century and was spread by the Prophet Muhammad. Islamic belief asserts that God sent more than one prophet to earth in order to teach the true way to eternal happiness in the next world. Moses and Jesus were two such prophets, who prepared the way for the final revelation of God's word through the Prophet Muhammad.

Islam is divided into two groups: the Sunni (SOON-nee) and the Shiites (SHEE-ites). The majority of Turks are Sunni, meaning that they follow the Sunna. The Sunna is the correct behavior exemplified by the life of Muhammad as it was recorded in the Hadith (Hah-DEETH). The Hadith, which covers a variety of topics including codes of behavior, is as important to Muslims as the Koran, the holy book of Islam.

8

Turkey is officially a secular country with no official religion since the constitutional amendment of 1924. However, today more than 99.8 percent of the country is Muslim. The remaining tiny percentage of the population comprises of Christians and Jews.

The Five Pillars of Islam are duties that every Muslim must perform. They include: (1) a declaration of faith, (2) daily prayers, (3) paying a special tax, (4) fasting, and (5) a pilgrimage.

- *The first pillar, the shahadah (shah-HAH-dah), or declaration of faith, is the deeply felt recital of the creed: "There is no god but God," and "Muhammad is the Messenger of God."*

- *The second pillar, the formal prayer to God, must be carried out five times a day at fixed hours, and always said while facing the direction of Mecca. This is why, in many Turkish hotel rooms, a small arrow on the ceiling indicates the direction of Mecca. Prayer time lasts about 20 minutes and usually occurs at dawn, after midday, in the late afternoon, after sunset, and after dark. It is not unusual to find a small blackboard outside a mosque with the exact times of prayer listed, for they vary slightly according to the time of year.*

- *The duty to fast during the month of Ramadan, known as Ramazan in Turkey, constitutes the third pillar.*

- *The fourth pillar involves paying a religious tax to help the poor and needy.*

- *The fifth and last pillar of Islam is the hajj. The hajj (HAHJ) is the annual pilgrimage to the holy city of Mecca. Every devout Muslim aspires to be able to make the pilgrimage at least once during his or her lifetime.*

The Shiites pay particular regard to the Prophet's son-in-law, Ali. The Shiite tradition includes an emphasis on sacrifice and martyrdom. Shiites also believe there is a hidden inner meaning to the Koran.

One group of Shiite Turks is the Alevi, a sect whose members live primarily in southeastern Turkey and western Syria. The Alevi are a group divided from the majority of Turks by their religion. The social rift between Alevis and Shiite Turks widened because the majority of Alevi live in enclosed areas, physically separated from the Shiites.

A visitor to Turkey is most likely to encounter the presence of Islam through the call to prayer from the *muezzin*, the Muhammadan crier who proclaims the hours of worship from the minaret of a mosque.

Opposite: Shiite Muslims in Istanbul mark the death of Imam Husayn, the grandson of the prophet Mohammed

THE PROPHET MUHAMMAD

The Prophet of Islam was born into a poor family in Mecca in A.D. 570. His parents died when he was five or six years old, and his relatives took care of him until he became a shepherd. As a young man, he earned the title of al Quraish, meaning the trustworthy. He married a wealthy widow who was his employer at the time. From A.D. 613, he began to spread the message of his revelations, denouncing all forms of idolatry. He never claimed to be more than the messenger of God as he went about Mecca preaching the virtues of a humble and sober life.

The severity of his attacks on the behavior of Mecca's citizens eventually contributed to his decision to flee the city. His secret departure from Mecca is known as the hijra (hi-JI-ra), after the Arabic word for the breaking of ties. He established the first Muslim community at Medina, and lived to see his religion reach Mecca when he took the city in A.D. 630. He died two years later in A.D. 632.

THE KORAN

The Koran is to Muslims as the Bible is to Christians. Muslims believe the Koran contains the words of Allah, which they believe were dictated to the Prophet Muhammad in Arabic by the Archangel Gabriel. The Koran is so holy that any questioning or criticism of it is thought to be a sacrilegious act. The words revealed to Muhammad are grouped into 114 chapters, known as *surahs* (SOO-rahs). They are not all concerned with matters of doctrine, but touch on many aspects of social life as well.

Religion **79**

Muslims praying in Selimiye Mosque in Edirne. They are required to worship five times a day.

The Ramazan fast is observed annually during the ninth month of the Muslim year. Between the hours of dawn and dusk, Muslims are forbidden to consume any food or drink. This prohibition also extends to smoking. During the time of Ramazan, newspapers carry details of the exact times of sunrise and sunset.

Although translated versions in many different languages have appeared, the Koran is considered untranslatable, and is only meant to be read in its original Arabic form. A supreme achievement for any Muslim is to learn the entire contents of the book by heart. When the Koran is transmitted by radio or television, it is read in more of a chant than speech. Readers of Arabic are drawn by the incantatory and poetic qualities of the text.

The Koran teaches that God is omnipotent. Those who obey the will of God will be judged favorably on the day of resurrection. Those who have sinned and do not repent for their wrongdoing will be condemned to eternal damnation in hell.

THE MOSQUE

The mosque is the Muslim place of worship. It is usually a fairly simple structure consisting of a large prayer hall. Toward the front of the prayer hall is the *mimber* (MIEM-behr), a kind of pulpit where the imam (ee-MUM), or prayer leader, sits or stands. Apart from the *mimber*, the only other essential aspect of the mosque is the mihrab (meh-RUB), a prayer niche in the wall showing the direction of Mecca. Outside the mosque, there is usually a tall, slim tower, the minaret, from which the call to prayer is made. An outer courtyard serves as a gathering space during religious festivals or a spillover area when the prayer halls become too crowded.

Ideally, a Turk will visit a mosque five times a day for the necessary act of prayer. But this is not something prescribed by religious law, and the ordinary

Turk will not feel obliged to seek out a mosque a set number of times each day. Muslims may pray at home or at their workplace at the appointed prayer times. Muslim women are permitted to visit a mosque to pray, but they are usually segregated from the men.

Unlike Christianity, Islam has no formal Mass or ceremony associated with the mosque. Islam also forbids the pictorial representation of Allah, people, or animals. As a result, the walls of a mosque may be decorated with geometric patterns, Islamic calligraphy of Koranic verses, or just left completely bare.

The only customary time when Muslims gather is for the Friday midday prayers. The imam leads the congregation in prayer. Worshippers prostrate themselves with their forehead touching the floor. The floor of the mosque is always kept clean and is covered with prayer mats or rugs.

Ritual ablution, or ceremonial washing, accompanies the five daily prayers. In larger mosques, an ablution fountain is found in the forecourt of the building. In smaller mosques, it is likely to take the form of a simple faucet above a basin in a wall near the entrance.

The Süleiymaniyae Mosque is considered the most beautiful of all imperial mosques in Istanbul. Built between 1550 and 1557 by Mimar Sinan, it contains the tombs of Süleyman the Magnificent and his wife. There are 200 windows; 138 are stained glass designed by an artist known as Ibrahim the Drunkard.

ATATÜRK AND RELIGION

Atatürk's aim was to modernize his country and break down the cultural barriers that isolated Turkey from the rest of Europe. Inevitably, this meant confrontation with Islamic beliefs and practices that he believed inhibited progress. Atatürk did not shy away from the enormity of his task when he set about divorcing religion from the state. Religious education in schools was brought to an end. Even his attack on the fez, and its replacement by the European hat, was seen as a symbolic blow to Islamic tradition. The fez, possessing no brim, facilitated the ritual act of bowing to the ground, whereas a hat would have to be removed before the ritual prostration. Women were also banned from wearing headscarves in government institutions and schools.

Atatürk's reform of the legal system in Turkey was more than symbolic. In keeping with religious tradition, the laws of the Koran had been the laws of Turkey. Atatürk replaced Islamic law with a legal system based on a Swiss model.

An imam praying in a backlit window in a mosque in Turkey.

Shoes are never worn in a mosque. At larger mosques, especially the ones that attract tourists, slippers or overshoes are provided for visitors. Women normally cover their heads before entering, and both men and women refrain from exposing their legs.

Inside a mosque, the words of the first pillar of Islam may be found painted or inscribed on the wall: "There is no god but God," and "Muhammad is the Messenger of God." Mosques are sometimes brightly decorated on the outside with strings of colored lights that spell out Koranic messages.

THE IMAM

The term *imam* has two different meanings for Muslims. Among Shiites, the imam can be a charismatic leader regarded as a supreme source of spiritual authority. In the more general sense, imam describes the officiating prayer leader of a mosque who is particularly learned in the traditions of Islam. Islam, unlike Christianity or Judaism, does not possess an institutionalized clergy; the imams are the closest equivalent.

Some act as full-time officials and take on the responsibility of an entire mosque. Others work only part-time, and may have jobs outside the mosque.

MODERN TURKEY AND ISLAM

The overwhelming majority of Turkey's citizens identify themselves with Islam, but Turkey is one of the more relaxed countries in the Muslim world. The religious ban on alcohol is commonly disregarded. In fact, the national drink *raki* (rah-KUH), contains alcohol, and beer is readily drunk. The ban on the eating of pork, however, is strictly observed.

Konya's famous green-tiled Mevlâna museum houses the mausoleum that attracts Sufi pilgrims from all over the Middle East.

In recent years, a resurgence of Islamic fundamentalism has had a great effect on the Turkish people, although perhaps not to the same extent as it has in some neighboring Muslim countries. In 1989 a law was passed that allowed women to wear head coverings while attending universities. Gestures like these contradict the spirit of Atatürk's secularization. Despite the resurgence of Islamic practices in the country, Turkey remains a non-Islamic state; it is neither governed by Islamic law nor administered through Islamic social institutions. Islam and politics are separated. From the 1980s, the role of religion in the state has been a divisive issue, as influential factions challenged the complete secularization called for by Kemalism and the observance of Islamic practices experienced a substantial revival.

SUFISM

The popular stereotype of Islam is that of a strict religion that forbids any exuberant display of emotion, tending to be legalistic in nature, and emphasizing religious prohibitions that restrict individual expression.

Sufism, a mystical movement that emerged throughout the Islamic world sometime in the 12th century represents a dramatic contrast to this image. Sufism emphasizes the need to relate to God in one's own personal way. Sufis believe that an individual can commune with God directly. The word comes from the Arabic word suf (SOOF), meaning wool, because the early storytellers wore clothes made of wool, and it is from them that Sufism descended. Dervishes are Sufis, known for their ecstatic rituals of prayer. Sufi sects have a variety of rituals, but their dances distinguish them most from mainstream Muslims.

THE WHIRLING DERVISHES

Members of the sect known as the Whirling Dervishes seek to attain an ultimate state of mystical communion with God. A stringed instrument called the *ney* (NAJJ), which the dervishes believe sounds like the voice of God, accompanies the dance. A dancer, who can be male or female, will typically dress in a jacket over a long, white robe that reaches to the ankles and flares out as the dance gathers momentum.

Throughout the dance, the right arm is held up to the sky, and the left arm is pointed downward. This stance represents the way in which grace comes from God and is passed down to people on earth. As the dancers turn

Whirling dervishes twirl and dance in order to achieve a mystical union with God.

and whirl, they repeat a chant under their breath. The musicians also sing a hymn that extols the virtues of seeking a mystical union with God. The dance itself has three clearly defined stages: knowledge of God, awareness of God, and union with God.

Traditionally, a white cone-shaped hat made from camel's hair is worn. This is taken to represent a tombstone and, hence, death. The jacket represents the tomb. During the course of the dance, the jacket is taken off and thrown aside. This symbolizes casting away earthly existence. The music is seen as the music of the heavenly spheres, and the revolving, dancing figures represent the heavenly bodies themselves. That is why the dancers always rotate in a counterclockwise motion. A Sufi poet has tried to express the philosophy behind the dance:

A portrait of the Mevlana, Jalal al-Din al-Rumi.

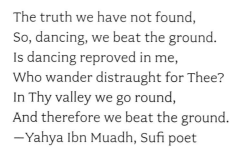

The truth we have not found,
So, dancing, we beat the ground.
Is dancing reproved in me,
Who wander distraught for Thee?
In Thy valley we go round,
And therefore we beat the ground.
—Yahya Ibn Muadh, Sufi poet

At the time of Atatürk's reforms, the order of dervishes came under attack as a typical example of the outmoded religious beliefs that were seen to hold back the development of a new and modern Turkey. A law was passed and enforced making it illegal for anyone to wear religious dress in public. This effectively outlawed the whirling dervishes, sending the movement underground. Today, a performance of the dance is officially permitted in Konya during the annual Mevlana Festival. The dancers are not only Turks, but include Sufi adherents from neighboring Muslim countries as well. The festival commemorates the anniversary of the death of Jalal al-Din al-Rumi on December 17, 1273. Better known as the Mevlana, which comes from the Arabic word for master, al-Rumi founded the sect of the Whirling

"Come, come whoever you are, whether you be fire worshipers, idolaters, or pagans. Ours is not the dwelling place of despair. All who enter will receive a welcome."
—Jalal al-Din al-Rumi, the Mevlana.

Jalal al-Din al-Rumi was a Persian born in 1207 in what is now Afghanistan. His father was a famous theologian who was invited by the Turkish sultan to live in the province of Konya in central Anatolia (below). Al-Rumi grew up in Konya and developed his own religious philosophy, while never abandoning the basic tenets of Islam. His work earned him the prestigious title of the Mevlana.

Al-Rumi preached the need for a universal and nonsectarian form of divine love. He criticized slavery and the practice of polygamy, and urged a more egalitarian role for women in many aspects of life. Humility was valued as a way of reaching truth. The most dramatic departure from orthodox Islam was in the promotion of dance and music as a means of perceiving beauty and achieving union with God.

The town of Konya is the repository of the original illuminated Mathnawi, the poetical work of al-Rumi. It has been translated into 12 languages. The museum in Konya also contains many of the priceless gifts received by al-Rumi during his own lifetime. One of the most famous is a 500-year-old carpet woven from silk. It is supposed to have taken five years to weave and was presented to the Mevlana as a gift from Persia.

Dervishes. The town of Konya has become the center of Sufi mysticism in the Middle East. Within Turkey, it has a reputation as a place of religious zeal and conservatism.

MAGIC

A belief in magic predates the country's conversion to Islam. Vestiges of a belief in supernatural powers can still be found in Turkey today. In the countryside of Anatolia, various small rituals are performed to ensure a plentiful supply of water. A scorpion is sometimes pinned to a tree, or a prayer written on a piece of paper is attached to the head of a dog before it is thrown into the water.

Blue beads are often associated with good magic, and it is not uncommon to see a string of blue beads hanging inside trucks and buses. People sometimes attempt to secure good fortune by carrying a magical charm, called a *muska* (m-OO-ska). This often takes the form of a small piece of paper with words from the Koran inscribed on it in tiny handwriting.

A tree hung with *nazar* charms in Cappadocia. These amulets are believed to protect against the evil eye.

INTERNET LINKS

www.turkeytravelplanner.com/go/CentralAnatolia/Konya/mevlevi.html

A fascinating page on the whirling dervishes (Mevlevi).

www.turkishodyssey.com/turkey/culture/religion.htm

A comprehensive page on Islam and the role of religion in modern-day Turkey.

www.enjoyturkey.com/info/facts/religion.htm

The history of the secularization of Turkey, together with facts about other religions in Turkey.

LANGUAGE

Local men chatting at a traditional cafe. Turkish is spoken by some 250 million people in the world.

9

TURKEY HAS NEVER been an isolated culture, so it should come as no surprise that Turkish has been influenced by many different linguistic heritages. Turkish is not a difficult language to learn. The spelling is basically phonetic, meaning fixed symbols always represent the same sound. Turkish is the first language for 83 million people around the world.

The roots of the Turkish language can be traced to Central Asia, with the first known written records dating back nearly 1,300 years.

A signboard in Turkey. Turkish is a phonetic language. Once the basic differences between the pronunciation of Turkish words and English words are mastered, it is not too difficult to read Turkish—even if not every word is understood!

ALTAIC AND URALIC

Altaic and Uralic are the names of two different language families that best describe the nature and history of the Turkish language.

Altaic (al-TAY-ik) is a family of some 50 languages, whose origin is believed to be in the Altay Mountains of Central Asia. Other Altaic languages include Mongolian, Korean, and Manchu-Tungus. Manchu was once the common language used between China and the outside world, and it may have been a language similar to Manchu that the Turks brought with them when they moved West. Manchu is rarely heard today.

Resemblances have also been found between Turkish and the Uralic languages such as Finnish and Hungarian. As with these languages, Turkish is based on a set of fundamental root words to which suffixes are added in order to change the nuance or define the meaning more precisely. The Uralic languages have been traced back to a region in the Ural mountains in the former Soviet Union.

Decorative and symbolic Arabic script is seen in many historical sites in Turkey; this piece is found in Tokapi Palace.

THE ARABIC CONNECTION

Turkish has been deeply affected by its exposure to the languages spoken in neighboring Arab countries, especially Persian (Iranian) and Arabic. This influence was particularly pronounced during the time of the Ottoman Empire. Indeed, for over one thousand years, Turkish was written using the Arabic alphabet. It was not until Atatürk began his radical reforms that Arabic script was suddenly replaced by the Latin alphabet, and Atatürk personally traveled throughout Turkey explaining and teaching the new alphabet to the people.

Good morning	Günaydin (*gerh-AYD-en*)
Good night	Iyi Geceler (*I-gi tel-ERH*)
Sorry	Affedersiniz (*a-fahl-as-IZ*)
Please	Lütfen (*lukh-VEN*)
Yes	Evet (*EV-et*)
Hello	Merhaba (*mer-HAB-ber*)
I don't understand	Anlamadim (*am-LAM-ah-dam*)

At the time, this change caused controversy and consternation across the country. Concern was due more to religious reasons. The Koran, which believers say is untranslatable, was originally written in Arabic. Abandoning Arabic script, it was thought, would lead to the weakening of the tie between Turkey's religion and culture.

Atatürk also set about purging Turkish of many of its Arabic and Persian words. Thousands of Arabic and Persian words had found their way into the Turkish language, because of the common Arabic script. Atatürk had many of these words replaced by new Turkish words. Sometimes, however, the new words bore a striking resemblance to their European equivalents. The Turkish word for school, for instance, became *okul* from the French *école*. The word for honor became *onur*.

NEWSPAPERS AND TELEVISION

There are more than a hundred newspapers and magazines, some online, available to the Turkish citizen. This is ironic given the Turkish government's track record of repressing freedom of the press through a mixture of intimidation, arrests, and financial machinations, including the sale in 2008 of a leading newspaper and a television station to a company linked to the prime minister's son-in-law.

The country has dozens of daily newspapers, both local and regional. *The Turkish Daily News* was the country's first English daily newspaper. The

Turkish is the official language of the country. Other languages spoken are Kurdish, Arabic, Armenian, and Greek. The Turkish spoken today evolved from Ottoman Turkish. Its origins, in turn, were from the language of the Seljuk Turks, Old Anatolian Turkish.

Newsstands cater
to a wide variety
of tastes; from
newspapers to
glossy magazines
to everyday
essential reads.

most popular and influential national newspapers, both domestically and internationally, are the liberal *Cumhuriyet* (Republic) and the politically independent *Milliyet*. Newsstands in the main Turkish cities, such as Istanbul and Ankara, carry a variety of foreign magazines and newspapers, such as the *Wall Street Journal*.

Until recently both television and radio were controlled by the state, but in July 1993, state monopoly was abolished. Turkish airwaves are lively, with some 300 private TV stations—more than a dozen of them with national coverage—and more than 1,000 private radio stations competing with the state broadcaster, Turkish Radio and Television (TRT).

Istanbul is the
media capital,
hosting the main
press outlets.
The city is home
to some 40 major
dailies with
nationwide reach
and 30 provincial
publications.

TURKISH VIA TELEVISION

The age of satellite television and private television companies has made a fresh range of Turkish-language programs available to Turkish people. There are hundreds of licensed channels not under the direct control of the government, although they are carefully monitored.

Currently new laws permit the broadcast of programs in non-Turkish languages. TRT has introduced broadcasts in Kurdish, banned for many years, under reforms intended to meet EU criteria on minorities. Kurdish-language TRT 6 TV launched in 2009. Satellite television has also brought English-language programs into people's homes, although these are usually subtitled. Some critics fear that traditional Turkish and Islamic values are being undermined as a result of such Western programs. CNN Turk and NTV (MSNBC) are also national television stations.

MINORITY LANGUAGES

Turkish is spoken by well over 90 percent of the population, making Kurdish the only significant minority language. Arabic can also be considered a minority language, although it is spoken by only 1 percent of the population and is only likely to be heard in the parts of southeastern Turkey that border Syria.

In the larger cities Greek and Armenian are sometimes heard. More common, however, would be English or French. *The Turkish Daily News* is printed in English, and the news is broadcast in English, French, and German on the national radio network.

INTERNET LINKS

www.turkeytravelplanner.com/details/LanguageGuide/100words_lessons/

Easy Turkish lessons to facilitate anyone who wishes to travel around Turkey.

www.digitaldialects.com/Turkish.htm

Digital games to facilitate the learning of the Turkish language, including dialects.

http://cali.arizona.edu/maxnet/tur/

Lessons in basic Turkish from the University of Arizona, complete with audio fill-in-the-blank exercises.

Around 36 million Turks were online by June 2012. Websites are subject to blocking. These have included YouTube, which was banned over videos deemed to be insulting to the founder of modern Turkey, Kemal Atatürk. However, circumvention techniques and technologies are widely used.

ARTS

The Islamic decoration on the domes of the interior of Ayasofya. Large plates of Islamic calligraphy decorate the beautiful interior of Ayasofya.

10

TURKEY HAS A RICH artistic culture in the fields of art, music, and literature. Most of it is relatively unknown outside of Turkey, although the rich architectural heritage is appreciated by many visitors and tourists. More recently, exciting artistic endeavors have been made in the form of movies and novels.

Creating beautiful floral and geometric designs, exquisite Iznik tiles adorn the façade of the Rüstem Pasha Mosque in Eminönü, Istanbul. This impessive mosque was built in 1563 by the Ottoman imperial architect Mimar Sinan.

A unique blend of Baroque, Rococo and Neoclassical styles were synthesized with traditional Ottoman architecture to create the Dolmabahçe Palace, which served as the main administrative center of the Ottoman Empire from 1856 to 1922

The 16th and 17th centuries are generally recognized as the finest period for art in the Ottoman Empire, much of it associated with the huge Imperial court at Topkapı Palace.

Islam forbids the pictorial representation of the human figure. For a country like Turkey that has adhered to Islamic tradition for centuries, this has inevitably influenced the development of Turkish art. Artists have turned their attention instead to abstract designs and floral motifs.

CERAMIC ART

Ceramic art is one of Turkey's oldest art forms. The town of Iznik in western Anatolia started as an established centre for the production of simple earthenware pottery. In the second half of the 16th century, thanks to the patronage of the Ottoman sultans Selim I and Suleiman I, craftsmen in the town began to manufacture high quality pottery with a fritware body painted with cobalt blue under a colourless lead glaze. Their meticulous designs, combining traditional Ottoman arabesque patterns with Chinese elements, firmly established the potters of Iznik as world-class practitioners of their art. By the beginning of the 17th century, over 300 kilns were operating and the tiles produced there were distributed throughout the Ottoman Empire. However, by 1750, Iznik had declined in importance, and a neighboring town started producing inferior substitutes. Today, only genuine Iznik tiles are deemed works of art. These tiles can still be found decorating some of the finest mosques in Turkey with the most outstanding examples to be found in the Blue Mosque in Istanbul and the Green Mosque in Bursa.

MUSIC

It is not difficult to have access to music in Turkey, and popular commercial music is as ever-present as it is in the rest of the world. Turkish music can sound discordant and somber to a listener who is accustomed to more mainstream Western music.

Until recently, folk music was not written down, and the traditions were kept alive by troubadours. *Ozan* (oh-za-HAN), the folk music of Anatolia, is associated with the *asiks* (ah-SIKHS), folk poets whose name translates as the ones in love. They accompany their poetry with music played on the *saz* (SAHZ), a stringed instrument with a long neck and three sets of strings.

Ottoman military music evolved when the troops were going into battle. Military bands would compete with canon blasts, and create a huge din with clarinets, kettledrums, cymbals, and drums.

MEVLEVI MUSIC

The founder of the Whirling Dervishes sect, the Mevlana, influenced the music of Turkey in a creative and imaginative way because his call for a more personal relationship with God encouraged artistic expression. Members of the sect are called the Mevlevi, and their distinctive music is known as Mevlevi music.

An Ottoman Janissary music band performing at Bursa Castle.

The Ankara Flying Broom Women's Film Festival is Turkey's only festival devoted to Feminism and Gender Issues. The festival is held on an annual basis in Ankara. The festival aims to support young women in making their debut films and organizes workshops on scriptwriting and filmmaking.

STRINGED INSTRUMENTS

- **Kemençe** *(keh-MENEH-cheh)* This resembles a fiddle with an oblong body and a short neck. It is held vertically, and the three strings are played with a nylon bow.
- **Ud** *(uh-DEH)* This is a lute without a fret, which is the bar or ridge that is often found on stringed instruments that helps to position the fingers correctly. The ud *was played by women in the harem. The* ud *is very similar to the* oud, *an Arab musical instrument.*

Wind Instruments

- **Tulum** *(tuh-luh-muh)* This is a bagpipe found mainly in the east where Turkey borders Georgia. There are five finger holes for each of the two pipes that protrude from the goatskin bag. The bag is filled with air by the player through bellows so that the air passes through the pipes.
- **Mey** *(mey-EH)* This instrument, a hollow metal or plastic rod, resembles an oboe with a large reed, the vibration of which produces the sound as air is pushed through. The same instrument is called duduk *in parts of eastern Turkey.*

Percussion Instruments

- **Davul** *(dah-VU-leh)* The davul *is a large drum with two sides. Each side is played with a stick of a different length to produce different sounds.*
- **Kasik** *(kah-SUHKH)* This is a set of spoons, made either from wood or metal. It is played by dexterous hand movements that bring the faces of the spoons together.

An essential part of the dervish dance is music. Mevlevi devotees composed their own music to accompany the ritual of the dance. Indeed, these musical compositions rank as works of art, and can be found among the works of composers such as Kocek Dervis Mustafa Dede (17th century) and Dede Efendi (19th century). The music is soothing and relaxing.

Two of the most traditional Mevlevi instruments are the *ney* and the *kudum* (KUD-um). The *ney* is a bamboo flute with six finger holes, five holes in the front and generally one hole in the back. It is not an easy instrument to master, and skilled *ney* players are highly regarded. The other instrument, the *kudum*, is a small kettledrum. It is usually played in pairs.

SHADOW-PUPPET SHOWS

The shadow puppets of *Karagoz* (KARA-goz) and *Hacivat* (HAH-ja-vaat) are part of a traditional Turkish art form that was once popular as entertainment but is now in danger of dying out. Karagoz and Hacivat are bearded clown figures whose conversation often acts as a form of social and political comment.

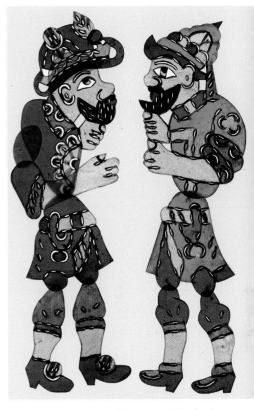

Figures of Hacivat (*right*) and Karagoz (*left*). Karagoz is often portrayed as the merry fellow, and Hacivat the prudent philosopher

The origin of these two characters is lost in legend. One popular account is that Karagoz was a blacksmith and Hacivat a stonemason, both employed by Sultan Osman in medieval times in the construction of a mosque. Their humorous conversations were so interesting that other workers stopped their work to listen. This incensed the sultan, who had them put to death, only to deeply regret the deed later. He found comfort in establishing a shadow-puppet show in honor of the two men.

A performance of a shadow-puppet show, often just called a Karagoz, consists of four parts. It starts in a Punch-and-Judy fashion with Hacivat being ridiculed by his colleague for speaking nonsense. This leads into the second part, where the puppet master displays his or her skill in manipulating the figures through improvisation. The conversation is also improvised as the humor becomes exaggerated. The conclusion of the show depends on the actual play chosen for a particular performance. In *The Treasure Hunt*, for

example, a minor character discovers a treasure in a well. When Karagoz searches in the same place, he only comes up with a crab, a dead mouse, and a bucket with holes in it.

Today, the most common reminder of this art form is found in the shadow puppets made in the likeness of the two characters. The figure of Karagoz is easy to recognize. He is always hunched over and dressed in brightly colored traditional Turkish dress with a turban on his head. Jointed pieces allow the turban to be flicked back, revealing his bald head.

A skilled puppeteer or *Karagözcü*. The lamp for projection is an oil lamp, while images are projected onto a white muslin screen known as the *ayna* (mirror).

Orhan Pamuk has sold over 11 million books in 60 languages, making him the country's best-selling writer. He has opened a "Museum of Innocence" in Istanbul.

Another jointed piece allows his hand to stroke his beard. Hacivat marionettes portray him as a more serious fellow who strokes his curved beard and is dressed in bright colors.

The better quality puppets are made with the same care that went into the crafting of the figures used in the shadow-puppet shows of the past. They are shaped from camel skin and then stretched over a frame of thin wooden strips. Constant polishing and rubbing reduces the finish to a thin translucent surface that is then colored in the bright red, green, blue, orange, and yellow of Ottoman period dress.

TURKISH CINEMA

Turkish cinema came to the world's attention in the 1970s through the internationally famous works of Yilmaz Guney. Guney was imprisoned in the early 1970s following a military coup, and he began directing movies from his prison cell. He would write a script behind bars and give detailed instructions to other movie directors, who directed the movie according to his wishes. Interestingly, the movies he made during his time in prison are regarded as his best work. A common theme in his work is the dislocation of rural life brought about by the growth of cities.

His most famous movie is *Yol* (The Road). It traces the fortunes of five prisoners who are released from prison on a week's parole. Their behavior becomes a parable of life in modern Turkey and is critical of the way society expects people to behave. Before the movie was released in 1982, Guney escaped from prison and fled to France where he edited the film. His last movie, *Duvar* (The Wall), is a critique of authoritarianism in society. Guney died of cancer in 1984 at the age of 46.

The 1990s saw the spotlight on Turkish women directors, such as Yesim Ustaoglu. Her 1999 film *Journey to the Sun* won the Blue Angel Award for Best European film. While at the Istanbul Film festival, Ustaoglu won Best Film, Best Director, and other prizes. In 2003, Cahide Sonku was honored in the Flying Broom Women's Film Festival. Sonku was Turkey's first female director. Another welcoming sign of progress has been the release of films dealing with political and social issues that were once censured.

Turkish filmgoers are pictured next to a poster of *Fetih 1453* or *Conquest 1453* at a cinema in Ankara. This 2012 film by Faruk Aksoy depicts the conquest of Istanbul by Ottoman Turks.

TURKISH WRITERS

Turkey has a number of prominent writers including Atilla Ilhan, Orhan Kemal, and Tarik Dursun K., but Yasar Kemal is perhaps Turkey's most famous writer. He was born in 1922 and began his career writing stories of rural life in Anatolia. His book *Memed* (My Hawk) won the 1996 Varlik Prize for the novel of the year and its translation into English was sponsored by UNESCO. His more recent works, *Saga of a Seagull* and *The Sea-Crossed Fisherman*, are concerned with the plight of the individual in the modern world.

Other writers concern themselves with themes that are considered sensitive and political by some people in Turkey. Irfan Orga's *Portrait of a Turkish Family* is a biographical account of growing up in Ottoman Turkey and coping with changes during World War I and the Westernization of the nation.

In 2003 Turkish writer Orhan Pamuk won one the world's richest literary prizes, the International IMPAC Dublin Literary Award. Pamuk was chosen by an international panel of judges for his work *My Name is Red*, a murder mystery story.

As a young man, Sinan served in the Ottoman Empire and had the opportunity to travel extensively through Eastern Europe and the Middle East. This not only opened his eyes to Islamic art but also the architecture of Christian lands, and he was able to absorb the best of both styles.

He first came to the attention of the sultan when his skill in designing military hardware such as bridges, siege machinery, and ships was recognized. He was appointed as chief architect to Süleyman the Magnificent. Based in Istanbul, Sinan was responsible for a number of small works before embarking on more ambitious projects that have earned him lasting fame. At the height of his fame, he traveled to Mecca and supervised the restoration of the Harem-i-Serif Mosque.

ART AND ARCHITECTURE

Turkey is greatly admired for its architectural style. The most celebrated architect of the Ottoman period was Mimar Sinan (1489—1588), who is best remembered for his masterpiece, the Süleymaniye Mosque in Istanbul.

SÜLEYMANIYE MOSQUE The roofs in this magnificent mosque complex dominate Istanbul's skyline. An elegant courtyard with columns of porphyry (a hard rock with white and red crystals), marble, and granite is found within the complex. There are four minarets and 10 balconies, all of which correspond to Süleyman's title as the fourth sultan and the 10th in line from Osman, the first Ottoman ruler.

The mosque is built in accordance with traditional Islamic principles. It lies beneath a grand central dome and has a strict geometric design; its height (174 feet or 53 m) is exactly twice its diameter, and it surmounts a square of exactly 87 feet (26.5 m). The mosque also features another traditional Turkish art—calligraphy. Calligraphy has been a major form of artistic expression in Turkey and Arab countries for centuries. Calligraphic inscriptions are written in Arabic, the language of the Koran, with elaborate decorations called arabesques.

AYASOFYA (HAGIA SOPHIA) The Ayasofya is another of Istanbul's architectural masterpieces. For nearly one thousand years, it held the title as the largest enclosed space in the world, an incredible achievement, since the building was commissioned in the sixth century. The construction of a dome spanning its diameter, measuring 31.87 m from north to south and 30.87 m from east to west and unsupported by solid walls on four sides, was an ambitious venture. The Byzantine church compares favorably with the great medieval cathedrals across Europe in the engineering skill, architectural design, and religious devotion that went into its construction.

Ayasofya was built as a church (Church of the Holy Wisdom), and after the Ottoman conquest of Constantinople in 1453 it was converted into a mosque. Sultan Mehmed II had a minaret erected on the southeast corner, and his successors added three more. Ayasofya functioned as a mosque until 1932 when Atatürk transformed it into a museum. Large medallions in the interior bearing calligraphic inscriptions of Allah, Muhammad, and the first four caliphs remind visitors of its Islamic heritage.

The Ayasofya was originally built as a church but later became a mosque. Today, it is used as a museum. One of the greatest surviving examples of Byzantine architecture, its interior is decorated with mosaics, marble pillars, and coverings of great artistic value.

TOPKAPI PALACE The mosques of Istanbul may signify the spiritual heart of Turkey, but Topkapı Palace represents the political power of the Ottoman state. The palace shows the same boldness of conception and marshalling of artistic talent that went into the religious buildings.

Following Islamic architectural tradition, the palace entombs a series of buildings that are surrounded by numerous courtyards. Work began on the first of four main courts in the mid-15th century. The first court was opened to the public as a general service area, while the second court was reserved exclusively for state functions. The third court housed administrative and bureaucratic officers and contained a school for the training of civil servants. The last court, surrounded by flowers, was designed for relaxation and pleasure.

The harem of Topkapı Palace is not the most important section architecturally, but it is definitely the building that attracts the most visitors. The largest number of concubines was said to be 809 during Sultan Abdülaziz's reign. Following a revolution in 1908, the harem was dissolved, and relatives of the slaves were invited to reclaim their kin and return them to their villages.

There are many priceless art objects from the Ottoman period kept in Topkapı Palace. The Topkapı dagger is famed for its three very large emeralds, one of which conceals a small watch. The palace also contains a valuable collection of paintings and miniatures dating from the reigns of Süleyman to Murad III. Sultans commissioned artists to illustrate their achievements, making these paintings notable for their depiction of human figures, although this is discouraged in Islamic art.

BLUE MOSQUE The mosque is so named because of the 20,000 blue Iznik ceramic tiles that line its interior. Officially called Sultanahmet Camii, which means Sultan Ahmet's Mosque, it was commissioned by Sultan Ahmet I in 1609. Architect Sedefkar Mehmet Agha took eight years to build the mosque, and when completed, it had six minarets instead of the usual four found in most mosques. This is believed to have been a result of a communication error between the sultan and the architect, who understood the sultan's request for gold minarets (altin) to mean six (alti) minarets.

The harem reception room in the Topkapi Palace. The word harem comes from the Arabic for "forbidden," and refers to the private rooms where the sultan's wives and concubines lived with their children.

INTERNET LINKS

www.last.fm/music/+free-music-downloads/turkish
Free downloads of contemporary Turkish music.

http://thehenrybrothers.wordpress.com/2012/01/26/karagoz-and-hacivat-shadow-theatre-a-turkish-storytelling-tradition/
A charming Karagöz and Hacivat story plot, complete with pictures and a youtube video.

www.turkishculture.org/architecture-403.htm
A page dedicated to Mimar Sinan's architecture, complete with seven pages of pictures.

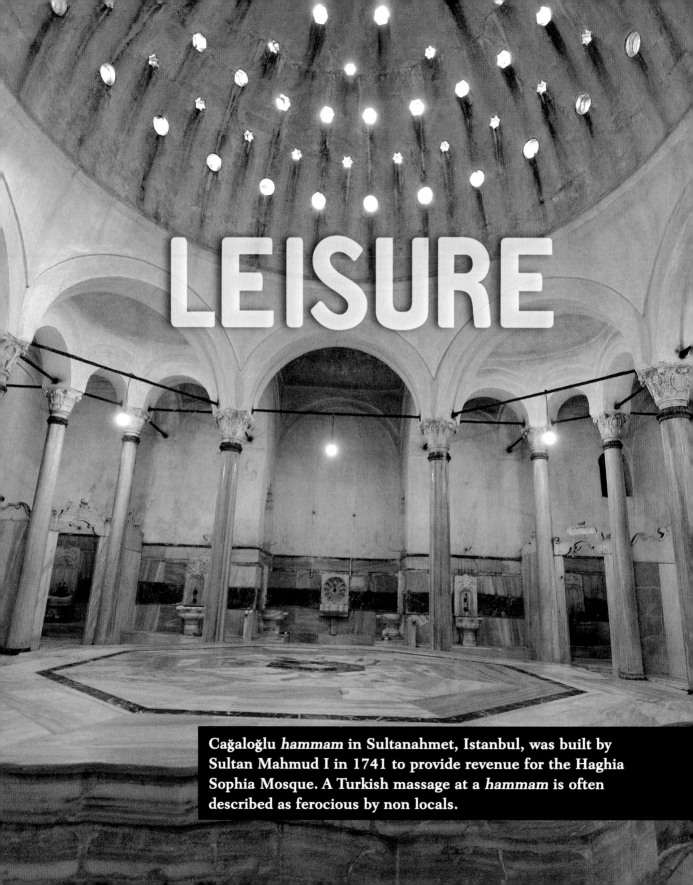

LEISURE

Cağaloğlu *hammam* in Sultanahmet, Istanbul, was built by Sultan Mahmud I in 1741 to provide revenue for the Haghia Sophia Mosque. A Turkish massage at a *hammam* is often described as ferocious by non locals.

TURKS ARE WELL AWARE of the importance of relaxing, and there is a strong tradition in the country of slowing down the pace of life in order to enjoy oneself with one's family.

In the home, television is becoming increasingly popular as a source of relaxation and leisure, and sports and other organized activities are common outside the home. Traditional forms of leisure include storytelling, playing a game of backgammon, greased wrestling, and visits to the Turkish steam bath.

HAMMAMS

A *hammam* (hah-MUM) is a Turkish steam bath, which is very much a part of Turkish life. Used by both men and women as a form of relaxation and personal hygiene, *hammams* are found even in small towns across the country. Sometimes the bathhouses will serve men and women on different days of the week, posting a schedule outside announcing which days are designated for which gender. Larger towns generally have separate *hammams* for men and women. Traditionally, *hammams* were heated by large wood-burning stoves, but today most bathhouses use electricity. Bathers pay a fixed fee to enter.

HAMMAM PRACTICES Visitors to a *hammam* usually bring their own soap and shampoo. Men are also required to bring their own shaving gear. For male bathers, the *hammam* provides a towel for the men to wear around their waists like a sarong. The *hammam* also provides guests with wooden clogs and a towel for drying off after the bath.

11

Traditionally, the masseurs in the baths were young men who helped wash clients by soaping and scrubbing their bodies. They were recruited from among the ranks of the non-Muslim subject nations of the Turkish Empire, for such work was considered to be beneath the dignity of a Muslim.

The central bath chamber is often very ornate. It is usually made of marble, and the numerous sets of basins and taps may be decorated with colored tiles of various design. Each visitor uses a separate basin, and in the men's locker room, there is an area designated for shaving after the main bath.

What distinguishes the *hammam* from a regular bath is the sauna-like *gobek tasi* (GO-bek TAA-shuh), or the naval stone, the warmest part of the room. A platform is placed above the stones, and men and women lie on it to absorb the heat the stones emanate. This is also the area where massages are usually administered. The Turkish masseurs and masseuses have a reputation for delivering vigorous massages.

Men smoking pipes, socializing, and enjoying coffee in a coffeehouse inside the Corlulu Mehmet Ali Pasa Medresesi in Istanbul. Even the smallest Turkish village has its coffeehouse where men talk, sip coffee, and hang out. For many men in Turkey, it is a good way to pass an afternoon.

SIMPLE PLEASURES

Most Turks enjoy relaxing and do not need television or highly organized activities in order to do so. It is common to see groups of people walking along the road chatting in larger cities like Istanbul or Ankara, or congregating in groups in smaller villages. A favorite pastime is to discuss politics or sports, and Sunday afternoons are often spent in this way.

Conversing over a cup of coffee or tea is more specifically a male form of leisure. Apart from modern cafés in the big cities that are frequented by both men and women, it is uncommon for women to socialize in this way. Men, however, will sit and talk for hours over tea at a small café. Often, there is a game of backgammon in progress, or a deck of cards will be made available by the proprietor for patrons to use.

It is still common to see men seated in a coffeehouse smoking their hubble-bubble pipes. These pipes, known as *nargile* (NAR-gil-eh) are often bought by tourists as souvenirs. To use them properly, compressed Persian tobacco must be packed into the pipe, and live coals dropped into the brazier end. This ensures a constant flow of smoke, which is contentedly puffed by coffeehouse patrons. A single match applied to regular pipe tobacco is said to be unable to achieve the same effect.

BACKGAMMON

Backgammon is deeply rooted in Turkish culture. It was introduced to Britain by the Crusaders, who learned the game from the Turks. Known as tavla *(TAV-lah) in Turkey, it is the country's most commonly played game. A backgammon set is easily purchased in almost any town. A set made from wood costs only a few dollars, but sets made of ivory and inlaid with mother-of-pearl can cost about $100.*

The game is played by two players, each of whom has 15 flat, round pieces that are organized precisely at the beginning of each game. The backgammon board is composed of two halves: the inner table and outer table. The object of the game is to move your own pieces after each throw of the dice around the board and home to your own inner table.

STORYTELLING

Turkey has a rich oral tradition of stories and legends that have been passed down from generation to generation. The origin of some of these tales goes back as far as the ancient days when the Turks were a nomadic race traveling westward from their homes in Central Asia before arriving in what is now Turkey. Although no written records remain from those times, it seems clear from some of the folktales that it was a violent age.

The hero in many of these stories is Dede Korkut and his band of loyal fighters. The legends, which are still relayed to Turkish schoolchildren through books, comics, and storytelling sessions, recount the heroic deeds of Dede Korkut against evil villains and thieves.

Most legends that are passed down orally are based on actual events. The myths of Dede Korkut are believed to be stories of the real-life exploits of a daring band of Turks who wandered westward from their home in Central Asia.

Even more famous than Dede Korkut is Nasreddin Hodja (NASS-rah-din HO-jah). The exploits of Nasreddin are well-known to nearly every Turk, and they have become a cornerstone of Turkish wit and wisdom. He was a 13th century philosopher who was able to defeat his opponents through his sharp tongue and quick wit. Like the court jester, he was able to get away with remarks that would have caused trouble for anyone else.

An Islamabad local dressed up as Nasreddin Hodja. Turkish legends are usually passed down from generation to generation through storytelling.

In one story, Hodja is the servant of a Tartar conqueror. One day, the conqueror cries aloud after catching sight of his ugly face in a mirror. Hodja joins in the crying and continues to do so even after the Tartar has stopped. When asked to explain, Hodja says, "If you, O great master, can cry for over an hour because you only catch a glimpse of your face in a mirror, then think of poor me who has to see your face every day."

Another often repeated story tells of the time Hodja talks to a friend about the creation of life. Hodja speculates that it would have been better if horses had been born with wings because that would make them far more useful to people. Just then, some pigeon droppings fall on his turban. Hodja stops for a moment, looks at the sky, and says, "Allah knows best!"

SOCCER

Soccer is the most popular sport in Turkey. Any town that can manage having a team will get a team together, which will be enthusiastically supported by the townspeople. A winning team's supporters are easily recognized; they

HODJA AND THE COOKING POT

One day, Hodja called at the house of one of his neighbors. He had a request to make.

"Could you please lend me one of your cooking pots? Mine is broken and needs to be repaired."

"Certainly," said his neighbor, who was pleased to hand over one of his biggest and best pots.

The following day, Hodja returned to his neighbor's house. When the door was opened, the neighbor was happy to see that the pot was being returned to him. Much to his surprise, there was another smaller pot inside the big one.

"Hodja, whose pot is this? You only borrowed my big pot. Where on earth did this small one come from?"

"Ah," replied Hodja in a matter-of-fact tone, "I forgot to tell you that while the big pot was in my house, it had a baby."

The neighbor was expecting to see Hodja smile, but he seemed quite serious. The neighbor decided to adopt a similar tone and replied that the news was unexpected but welcomed.

Some time passed and nothing more was ever said on the subject. Then a time came when Hodja called once more at his neighbor's house and asked to borrow a cooking pot. Again, the pot was willingly given to him. This time, however, Hodja did not return to the house. After a while, the neighbor grew anxious and, eventually, decided to call on Hodja himself to ask for the return of the pot. Much to his surprise, Hodja politely informed him that he no longer had the pot.

"What?" said the concerned man. "Are you saying you lost my best pot?"

"No, I would not be so careless as to lose your best pot. I am afraid something very unfortunate has happened."

"What has happened to my pot?" demanded the neighbor, who was beginning to feel angry.

"Your pot became seriously ill and died, I am afraid to say," replied Hodja in his most serious tone of voice.

"Died! My pot has died, you say. What do you take me for? A fool? Do you seriously expect me to believe that my cooking pot is dead?"

Hodja looked him in the eye and replied, "Well, you were quite ready to accept that your pot had a baby, weren't you? So why is it so difficult to believe that it is now dead?"

Children enjoying a soccer game on the streets of Istanbul.

are often heard before they are seen. The incessant honking of car horns is a characteristic sign of victory.

Soccer has led to all kinds of gambling on a national scale. It is not confined just to local matches, but has been organized into a system that attracts fans across the country. Because large sums of money are involved, there have been cases of bribery involving players and managers who attempt to fix the outcome of a league game in exchange for a payoff.

In 1995 Turkey announced its arrival on the international soccer scene when it reached the finals of the European soccer championship. In the 2002 World Cup, Turkey not only reached the semifinals, but beat co-hosts South Korea 3—2, finishing in third place. The team's performance exceeded expectations, and thousands of fans packed the streets of Istanbul to welcome the team home. Turkey finished third again in the 2003 Confederation Cup and qualified for the Union of European Football Associations (UEFA) Euro 2008.

GREASED WRESTLING

Wrestling has been a popular sport among Turkish men for centuries. Turkey nearly always enters a team in the Olympics. But one form of wrestling has not yet found its way into the Olympic Games. This is Turkish greased wrestling. Contestants wear nothing but tight leather breeches called *kisbet* (KIZ-but). Their bare bodies are rubbed with diluted olive oil, making it difficult for the opponents to maintain a hold on each other.

Contestants in greased wrestling are grouped by height rather than weight. Competitive matches follow strict rules and are usually explained thoroughly by a master of ceremonies, invariably a former champion of the sport. The referee's task is to watch carefully for any illegal move. The actual duration of any one match can be anywhere from one or two days. As in mainstream wrestling, the winner must pin his opponent to the ground for a specified number of seconds. The most prestigious wrestling event, the Kirkpinar Festival, takes place in July each year.

OTHER TURKISH SPORTS

CIRIT (jer-IT) This is a traditional Turkish sport that is becoming increasingly rare. It is played during the winter on horseback. The rider carries a blunt wooden javelin. The objective of the game is to throw the javelin hard enough and accurately enough to hit the opponent. Each hit earns a player one point, and the winner is the rider who first achieves the set number of points.

HUNTING AND SHOOTING This was once more than just a sport, as game was a valuable source of food for peasants. A notable exception to this is boar hunting, because Muslims do not eat pork.

SKIING Turkey is not usually associated with skiing, but the country's many mountains allow for good skiing. About 16 ski resorts have opened in different parts of the country, each with varying levels of difficulty and terrains. December to April is the best season for skiing.

Cirit, the "javelin game" of daredevil horsemanship, is a sport where wooden javelins are thrown at horsemen of the opposing team to gain a point. The game is played mainly in eastern Turkey.

INTERNET LINKS

www.passportchop.com/europe/turkey/turkish-bath-massage-hamam/

A great description of a Turkish Bath and massage, complete with a video of Michael Palin having a Turkish bath.

www.turkishculture.org/lifestyles/turkish-culture-portal/cirit/the-traditional-game-329.htm

A write up about the traditional game of cirit, including a video.

http://bigloveturkey.com/culture/festivals-kirkpinar-wrestling.asp

A write up about the Kirkpinar oil wrestling festival complete with pictures.

Hundreds of barrels of olive oil are poured over the wrestlers at Kirkpinar each year.

FESTIVALS

A festival is staged in a historical site in Turkey, whereby the backdrop lends a sense of drama to the performance. Festivals in Turkey are invariably accompanied by music and dancing—each region in Turkey has its own special folk dance and costume.

12

TURKEY CELEBRATES A number of interesting cultural festivals every year, but two of Turkey's most important festivals are religious in nature. One marks the end of Ramazan (Ramadan), the most significant event in the Muslim calendar, while the other marks the end of the pilgrimage to Mecca. Both are public holidays, and shops, banks, schools, and offices can be closed for up to four days.

In addition to the religious events, there are a number of interesting cultural festivals, such as the one dedicated to greased wrestling that takes place near Edirne every year in the early summer.

SEKER BAYRAMI

Seker Bayrami is the celebration marking the end of Ramazan, the Muslim period of fasting that lasts one month. During the month of Ramazan, no food or drink is allowed to be consumed between sunrise and sunset. The end of the long fasting period is celebrated with family feasts where special sweets are distributed to children. Provincial Turkish cities still celebrate this religious holiday in the traditional manner. Town elders dance to traditional music and greased wrestling matches are held.

More than 100 festivals are held in Turkey every year. Along with festivals of local scale held in almost every city of the country, cultural events and other festivals of international reach are also organized in major metropolitan centers such as Istanbul, Ankara, İzmir, and Antalya.

Men battle it out at the Kirkpinar Festival, or Turkish oil-wrestling tournament—an annual tradition in Edirne since 1346.

The time for Kurban Bayrami is determined based on the lunar calendar. Since the lunar year is ten days shorter than the year based on the sun, the time for Kurban Bayrami goes back ten days every year.

KURBAN BAYRAMI

Kurban Bayrami is also known as the Feast of the Sacrifice. Many Turkish families commemorate the day by slaughtering a sheep. The killing of the animal mirrors a story told in the Koran in which Ibrahim (Abraham) sacrifices a sheep in place of his son Ishmael (Isaac). The Judeo-Christian version similarly tells of how Abraham was willing to sacrifice his son, Ishmael, in obedience to God's command, and how God substituted a sheep at the last moment.

Buying an entire sheep for the sacrifice is too expensive for some families, and there is often too much meat left over so butchers now sell only part of a sheep around the time of the festival.

CULTURAL FESTIVALS

Every summer, the prestigious International Istanbul Festival takes place. Visitors come from all over the world, and top artists from East and West vie to appear in this month-long festival of the arts. Major events include performances of European and Turkish operas, ballet, and music. Part of the appeal of these performances is that they are staged in places such as the Topkapi Palace.

The Mevlana festival in Konya is the only time visitors and locals can see the whirling dervishes perform. When Turkey became a republic, all brotherhoods were outlawed and the Mevlevi were only allowed to resume their religious ceremonies once a year in Konya. The festival coincides with the anniversary of the death of the Mevlana.

KIRKPINAR FESTIVAL

The Kirkpinar Festival takes place every July in a small town near Edirne, very close to the Greek border. One of Turkey's oldest cultural festivals, it is a series of tournaments leading to the declaration of the greased wrestling champion of the year.

- *New Year's Day (January 1) This is a public holiday for Turkey.*

- *Seker Bayrami and Kurban Bayrami These two important religious events are fixed by the Muslim lunar calendar. This means that the exact dates vary from one year to the next.*

- *Kurdish New Year (March 21) The Kurds call this day* Newroz, *which means new day in the Kurdish language.*

- *National Sovereignty and Children's Day (April 23) This is the anniversary of the opening of the first Grand National Assembly in Ankara. Atatürk dedicated this day to the country's future —Turkey's children (above).*

- *Youth Day (May 19) This is the anniversary of Kemal Atatürk's landing at Samsun in 1919 at the beginning of his liberation movement in Anatolia.*

- *Victory Day (August 30) This marks Turkey's victory over the invading Greek forces in the 1922 War of Independence.*

- *Republic Day (October 28 and 29) Events on these days commemorate Atatürk's proclamation of the Turkish Republic.*

- *Atatürk's Death Anniversary (November 10) This is not an official public holiday, but places of entertainment are closed and alcohol is not sold for the day. Business carries on as usual until 9:05 A.M., when the whole country stops to observe 60 seconds of silence, to mark the hour of Atatürk's death.*

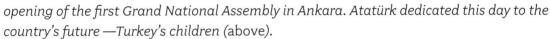

A popular story places the origin of the event to the time of Süleyman. Returning with 40 men from a battle in 1360, Süleyman chose to camp near Edirne. To pass the time, the men began wrestling in pairs. The two men who emerged as finalists were so equally matched that they wrestled until the pair collapsed in utter exhaustion and died. Buried by their comrades, they were forgotten until the following year when the graves were visited by some of Süleyman's men. On the site, they found 40 kirkpinar, or springs of fresh water.

THE WOODEN SPOON DANCE *Also called* Kaşık Oyunları, *this dance takes place in the area around the town of Silifke on the Mediterranean coast* (right). *Male and female dancers are dressed in the colors of the rainbow, and the rhythm is kept with a pair of wooden spoons that the dancers hold*

in their hands. The wooden spoons symbolize the woodworking tradition behind the people of Silifke. The dance usually tells a story about Turkey's early immigrants and how they lived and worked. The instruments used are beast bow (later violin), baglama *and clarinet, accompanied by folk songs.*

THE SWORD AND SHIELD DANCE OF BURSA *Also called* Kiliç Kalkan, *this dance represents the conquest of the city of Bursa by the Ottomans. The dancers are all men, dressed in the battle gear of the early Ottoman warriors. There is no musical accompaniment, only martial sound effects produced by the clashing of swords and shields as the dancers hurl themselves in the air.*

THE HORON DANCE *This distinctive dance is performed in the Black Sea coast area, where fishing is a common source of income. Dancers, all male, wear black clothes with trimmings of silver. They link arms and shake in a quivering motion to the vibrations of a local musical instrument that bears a resemblance to the violin. The sharp, wriggling movements imitate the movement of fish when caught and taken out of the water. The dance reflects the theme of fishing, which is an important aspect of the Black Sea culture.*

Now, over 600 years later, men still wrestle on that spot for the prestigious title of overall champion. As many as a thousand Turkish men flock to Kirkpinar to participate in the festival each year, and the finalists stand to win fame and fortune.

FOLK FESTIVALS

Folk festivals are held regularly in Turkey. Every region and most rural villages have their own folk dances and special costumes. There are many varieties of Turkish folk dancing. Both the dances and the accompanying music originated on the steppes of Asia before the Turkish groups converted to Islam.

Folk dances are characterized by exuberant movements. Unfortunately, in recent years, such events have become increasingly rare, but the remaining festivals provide a wonderful opportunity to see an integral part of Turkish village life.

Men dressed in the traditional Turkish Aegean military costume. In the *Zeybek* folk dance, these colorfully-dressed male dancers, called "*Efe*" symbolize courage and heroism.

The İzmir International Fair is the oldest tradeshow in Turkey, considered the cradle of Turkey's fairs and expositions industry. It is held every year in September.

INTERNET LINKS

www.dunav.org.il/balkan_music_turkish.html#all

A website with descriptions of the Turkish folk dances and musical scores, complete with playable MP3 files.

www.pilotguides.com/destination_guide/middle-east-north-africa/turkey/kirkpinar_wrestling_festival.php

A write up about the Kirkpinar Wrestling Festival, complete with pictures and all the technicalities of the contest.

www.lonelyplanet.com/turkey/travel-tips-and-articles/21114

An in-depth description of the Melvana festival, complete with pictures.

FOOD

A cook carves slices of lamb grilled on a vertical spit for *doner kebabs* in Istanbul. This favorite local dish can be found in many Turkish restaurants around the world.

13

FOOD IN TURKEY is associated with nearly every social event. Certain dishes are made especially for religious festivals and for important events like a child's first day at school, when it is customary to send a sweet called *lokma* (LOCK-ma) to the teacher. Traditionally, everyone in the family gets involved in elaborate food preparation.

Turkish cuisine varies between cities and rural areas. For example, the cuisine of Istanbul is more elaborate and refined, whereas traditional Turkish food is still being served in rural areas. Famous traditional soups, such as mother-in-law soup and brides' soup are associated with social events.

In recent years, serious chefs are re-emphasizing national dishes. Turkish cuisine is a source of national pride. For decades, the city of Bolu has held a national chef competition for the best Turkish chefs.

MEZE

Meze (MAY-zay) are Turkish *hors d'oeuvres* (small snacks served before the main meal) and are very popular during meals. *Sigara boregi* (see-GAH-rah bo-RAY-gee), for instance, is a tightly rolled cheese pastry. *Imam bayildi* (ee-MUM ba-YEEL-dee) is made from cooked eggplant filled with onions and tomatoes and served cold. *Imam bayildi* translates as the imam swooned, the suggestion being that the dish was so delicious, the imam, or prayer leader of the mosque, almost fainted at the sight and taste of it.

Turkish cuisine is largely the heritage of Ottoman cuisine, which can be described as a fusion and refinement of Central Asian, Middle Eastern, and Balkan cuisines.

Breakfast *A Turkish breakfast is a modest affair compared to the traditional American breakfast. It usually consists of bread, white cheese, and a few olives. Small cafés also serve borek (BEHR-rack), a pastry filled with bits of mincemeat or cheese, and a soup seasoned with lemon.*

Lunch *A favorite lunch is cabbage leaves stuffed with chopped meat and rice and served with yogurt. A form of pizza, known as pide (PEE-deh), is also eaten for lunch with various toppings of minced lamb, cheese, or egg.*

Evening Meal *This is the main meal of the day for most Turks. It often begins with a soup of rice and vegetables or lentils. The main dish might be shish kebab or perhaps chicken with rice. Although shish kebab is the most widely known Turkish dish, it is prepared in a variety of ways. Kebab dishes are usually eaten with pita bread.*

In the countryside, the evening meal is often based on boiled buckwheat served with fresh vegetables. This dish is known as bulgur pilavi (bool-GOOR PEE-lah-vih). Ayran (EYE-run), yogurt mixed with water and salt, is as common a drink in Turkey as sodas are in the West.

Meze are almost always served with raki (rah-KEY), the white Turkish national drink distilled from raisins and flavored with aniseed.

TURKISH DELIGHTS

There are significant regional variations in Turkish cuisine. Farming families in Anatolia have what is probably the least varied diet, being heavily dependent on buckwheat, soup, and stewed meat. The coastal area around the Black Sea, on the other hand, has the benefit of fresh anchovies and locally grown nuts. Walnuts are crushed, turned into a puree, and seasoned with pepper before being dripped over chicken. Known as Circassian chicken, this popular meze dish is appreciated around the world. The cooking of Istanbul, Bursa, Izmir, and the rest of the Aegean region inherits many elements of Ottoman court cuisine, with a lighter use of spices, a preference for rice over bulgur, and a wider use of seafood.

In the southeast, the proximity of Arab lands has influenced the choice and style of food. Chickpeas and other legumes, such as peas, beans, and lentils, are staples, and the kebabs are hotter and spicier.

Vegetables are not mere accompaniments to meat but are prepared and served as delicacies in themselves. Many vegetables, such as tomatoes, peppers, eggplants, pumpkins, and squash, are stuffed with rice and meat. If Turks want their vegetables served in this way, they will order *dolmasi* (doll-MAA-shee), which literally means stuffed.

With a ready supply of fresh fish, it is not surprising to find fish dishes served in a variety of ways. Any town near the coast will have a plentiful supply of fresh sardines and tuna. They are eaten as snacks or as a light lunch with thinly baked bread. Swordfish is often grilled on a skewer and mixed with pieces of pepper and onion. This swordfish kebab is called *kilicsis* (kihl-ITCH-shish).

A fish stand at a market in Istanbul. Surrounded on three sides by the sea, Turkey has an abundant supply of fish, and fishing is the chief means of livelihood for coastal dwellers.

Food   **123**

EGGPLANT AND YOGURT

Patlican (pat-la-JAN) or eggplant, is called the king of vegetables by Turks. There are said to be over a hundred recipes based on this vegetable. Some of them have interesting names, such as sultan beyendi (SOOL-tan bay-YEN-dee), which means "what is pleasing to the sultan."

Yogurt is a word that Turkey has contributed to the English language, and it is an ingredient in many meals and refreshments. One very tasty snack, called manti (MAN-tee), is a meat-filled ravioli that is soaked in yogurt and spicy oil.

FRIED EGGPLANT WITH YOGURT SAUCE

1 eggplant
pinch of salt
1 tablespoon lemon juice
olive oil
sauce (recipe follows)

Cut the eggplant into slices and lay them flat on the table before sprinkling with salt and lemon. Turn the slices over and repeat on the other side. Leave the eggplant slices for about 20 minutes, then drain and leave to dry. Heat the olive oil in a pan and, when hot, add the eggplant slices. Fry gently on each side for a couple of minutes. When the slices begin to turn reddish-brown, serve them on a plate with the yogurt.

YOGURT AND GARLIC SAUCE

8 fluid ounces (237 ml) plain yogurt
pinch of salt
1 clove garlic, mashed
pinch of ground black pepper
2 teaspoons olive oil

Whisk the yogurt in a bowl until smooth and creamy. Add all the remaining ingredients and beat in to mix thoroughly. Cover and keep cool while preparing the eggplant.

ETIQUETTE AND TABOOS

Etiquette allows, and sometimes expects, a customer in a *lokanta* (low-KANT-a), or restaurant, to go into the kitchen and inspect the food being prepared and cooked. There will usually be at least one large saucepan containing the main meat dish of the day, and it is perfectly acceptable to taste the food.

The only taboo that is widespread is eating pork. Islam strictly forbids the consumption of pork, and even cooking utensils should not be used if they have come into contact with the meat. Islam also prohibits the drinking of alcohol, but beer and wine are available and consumed by many Turks. There is no taboo about requesting an alcoholic drink.

In rural areas, unaccompanied women visiting social places are sometimes ushered either upstairs or behind a curtain on the same floor as the restaurant. Women are also not expected to visit a *meyhane* (may-HAH-nay), the Turkish tavern or pub. These places are reserved for men.

Diners at a restaurant in Bursa Street, Anatolia. For Muslims, eating pork is strictly forbidden.

TURKISH DELIGHT

½ cup (125 ml) rosewater

2 cups (500 ml) sugar

2 tablespoons (30 ml) gelatin

¼ cup (60 ml) cold water

½ cup (125 ml) orange juice

¼ cup (60 ml) lemon juice

confectioner's sugar

Mix rosewater with sugar in a saucepan, and heat to 255°F (105°C). Remove from heat. Soften gelatin in cold water for 5 minutes. Add the gelatin mixture to the cooked syrup. Add the juices and stir. Strain mixture through a sieve. Pour into a buttered 6" X 6" (15 cm x 15cm) square pan and let stand for about 2 hours or until the mixture is firm. Turn out and cut into squares. Roll in confectioner's sugar.

KEBABS

Lamb is the national meat of Turkey and its superior taste is due to the variety of herbs the lambs eat when they graze. Many recipes originated in pre-Islamic days when Turks lived a pastoral existence as shepherds and lamb was always available. Today, lamb is grilled, stewed, minced, or baked, but a national and international favorite is charcoal roasted cubes of lamb known as shish kebab. Lamb, beef, or chicken is seasoned with various spices, then compressed into a large inverted cone that is turned on a vertical rotating grill in front of hot coals. Another well-known kebab is the *doner kebab*. When a customer requests a

The southeast is also famous for its dough-based desserts such as baklava.

doner kebab, thin slices of garlic-flavored chicken are carved off the rotating grill and served with yogurt and cucumber on pita bread.

Besides being grilled as kebabs, lamb is also stewed or minced and made into meatballs, called *kofta* (KOFF-ta).

DESSERTS AND SWEETS

The true Turkish delights are the desserts and sweets. Afternoon teas accompanied by pastries and cookies are almost a ritual in Turkish homes. Baklava (BACK-la-va) is a typical treat that consists of small, thin pastry layers soaked in rich syrup with crushed nuts. There are many variations of this sweet mixture of sugar, flour, nuts, and butter. The window display of any *pastane* (pas-TARN-ee), or pastry shop, usually contains a tempting selection.

The Turks also bake a sweet pudding from a shredded chicken breast and rice mixture that is sprinkled with cinnamon and covered in milk. Other desserts that Turks love to prepare and eat are *lokma*, which are round doughnuts in syrup, *krem karamel* (caramel custard), and *kabak tatlisi* (slices of pumpkin in syrup).

DRINKS

Tea, called *cay* (CHA-hy), is grown along the Black Sea coast. It is prepared in an elaborate double boiler called a *samovar*, and poured into tiny glasses before being diluted to suit one's taste. It is usually served with sugar but never with milk. Shop owners make many sales by luring customers into their shops with offers of tea.

A traditional *samovar* in Cappadocia. Turkish tea is specially brewed over boiling water and served in small clear glasses. This allows the red color of the tea to be seen and keeps the tea hot for long periods.

Legend has it that Turks can tell your fortune by examining the residue of the coffee at the bottom of your cup. After consuming your coffee, cover your cup with a saucer and swirl it clockwise three times. Let the coffee settle for a while.

Your fortune can be told by reading the shapes formed from the residue. Some examples are: a claw means danger is ahead; a chair means an unexpected guest is coming; a fish means you will find wealth; beans mean financial trouble; a cat means a quarrel will soon happen; and a candle means that a friend will soon help you.

The position of the image is also important. If the shape is near the handle of your cup, then the prediction will happen near your home.

Although conservative Muslims campaign against the easy availability of alcohol, beer and wine are drunk throughout Turkey. There are vineyards across western Anatolia, and over a hundred varieties of red and white wine are available.

The most commonly drunk alcoholic beverage, however, is raki. It is the national aperitif (alcoholic appetizer) and is usually served with ice and diluted with water. Raki clouds over when water is added to it, giving it the popular name of *Aslan Su*, or lion's milk.

Muslims often drink *sira* (SEE-rah), a nonalcoholic grape drink. It is commonly available in restaurants that do not serve alcohol. There are many other traditional beverages. One that contains medicinal properties is salep (sah-LEHP). It is made from hot milk and the roots of a wild orchid found in the coastal areas of the country. Sprinkled with cinnamon, salep is a favorite remedy for a cold or the flu.

Raki, the national alcoholic beverage, is distilled from raisins, and aniseed is added to it. Raki is related to Greek ouzo and Arabic arrack.

TURKISH COFFEE

Coffee was first introduced to Europe by the Turks. When Ottoman invaders fled from Vienna after their failed attempt to capture the city, the Austrian defenders found barrels of coffee left behind. Turkish coffee, known as *kahve* (KAH-veh), is made from very finely ground coffee beans with just a touch of cardamom added. The flavor is thick and strong, so a generous amount of sugar is added. The heavy coffee grounds sink to the bottom of each cup and are not meant to be consumed.

To make authentic Turkish coffee, a *cevez* (jeh-VEZ-eh) is necessary. This is a narrow-necked, long-handled pot that helps create a froth. The coffee itself is served from demitasse cups that are about one-third the size of a regular coffee cup.

Turks distinguish between Turkish coffee and Western coffee, which they call *kahve ala frengi* (KAH-veh-ala-freng-EE).

A stall vendor preparing a cup of traditional Turkish coffee in Istanbul.

INTERNET LINKS

www.turkishfoodandrecipes.com/

A comprehensive recipe collection, complete with pictures and user comments.

http://mediterraneanturkishfoodpassion.blogspot.com

A lovely personalized blog about Turkish food with an impressive collection of recipes and beautiful pictures.

www.turkish-cuisine.org/english

What makes this Turkish recipe guide different is that it comes with a history of Turkish cuisine, and a guide to ingredients, together with the mandatory comprehensive recipe library.

Although Turkish coffee is renowned throughout the world because of its distinctive flavor, Turks drink more tea than they do coffee.

FRIED EGGPLANT SANDWICH

This dish can be served as a *meze*, or appetizer, or as a main course. Makes 2 servings

2 medium eggplants, sliced into ½-inch (1-cm) thick rounds

¼ cup olive oil

Salt and pepper to taste

8 ounces (240 g) grated Swiss cheese

3 tablespoons (45 ml) chopped parsley leaves

1 teaspoon (5 ml) dill

3 medium eggs, beaten

½ cup (240 g) plain flour, sifted

½ cup breadcrumbs

Cooking oil

Preheat the oven to 400°F (204°C). Coat the eggplant slices with olive oil, and place on a greased baking tray. Sprinkle with salt and pepper, and bake for 15 minutes. Remove from the oven, and set aside. Combine the cheese, parsley, dill, and half the egg. Sandwich a spoonful of the mixture between two eggplant slices, then brush with the flour. Dip in the remaining egg, and cover with breadcrumbs. Refrigerate the sandwiches for 30 minutes. Heat the cooking oil, and deep-fry the sandwiches until golden brown. Drain and serve hot.

LAMB KEBABS

This dish can also be served as a *meze* or as a main course. Makes 8 servings

4½ pounds (2 kg) of boneless lamb, cut into 2-inch (5-cm) cubes

Pinch of salt

1 medium onion, peeled and quartered

1⅓ cups (335 ml) olive oil

⅓ cup (85 ml) lemon juice

3 tablespoons (45 ml) garlic paste

3 tablespoons (45 ml) oregano

2 tablespoons (30 ml) ground black pepper

Sliced cucumbers, and tomatoes for garnish

Sprinkle the lamb cubes lightly with salt, and set aside. Blend the onions in a blender to form a fine paste. Add the olive oil, lemon juice, garlic paste, oregano, and black pepper, and blend well. Marinate the lamb cubes with the blended mixture, and leave in the refrigerator for at least one night. Remove the lamb cubes from the marinade, and skew the cubes on a metal skewer. Grill or barbecue the lamb kebabs until cooked. Serve with tomato and cucumber slices on rice or bread.

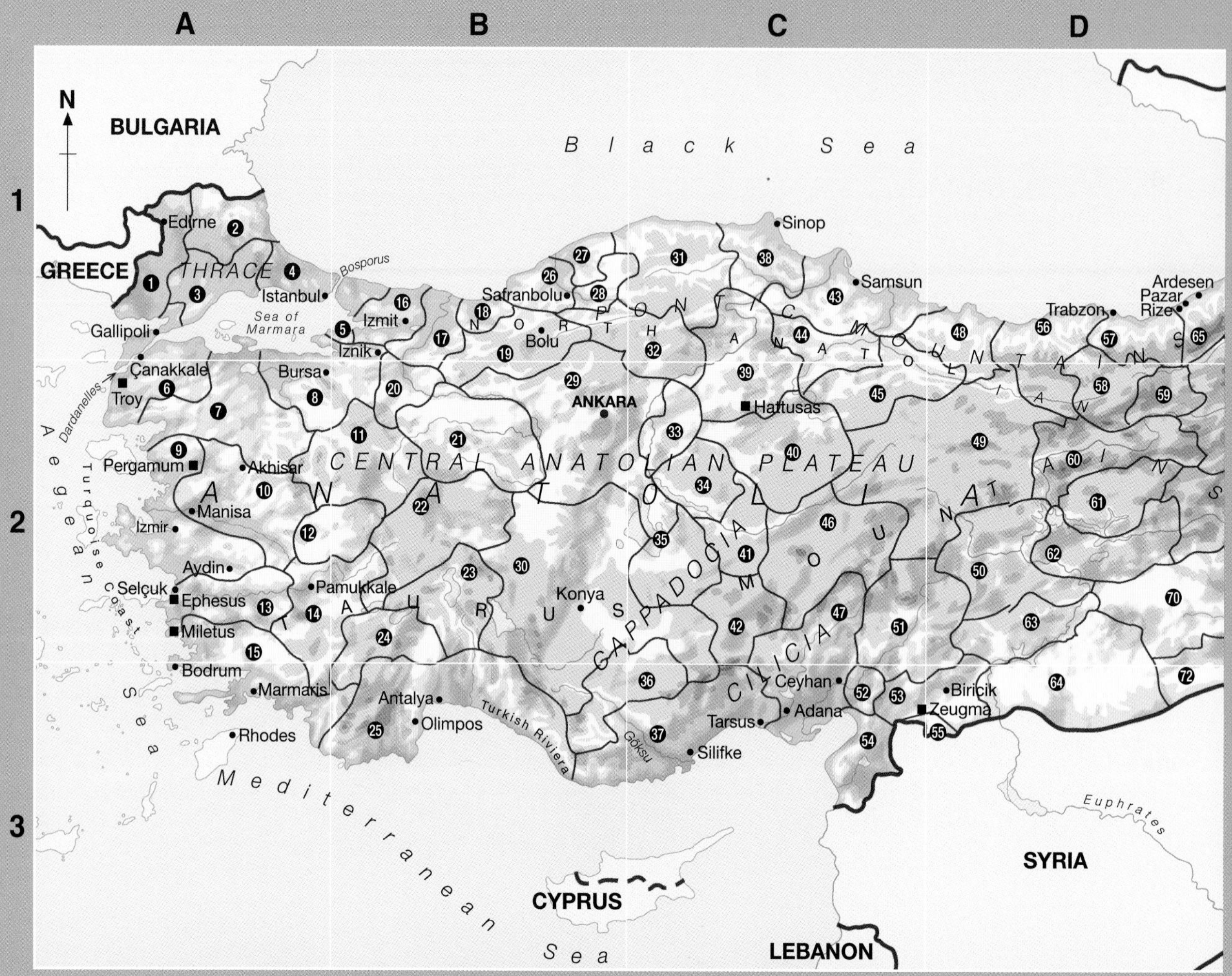

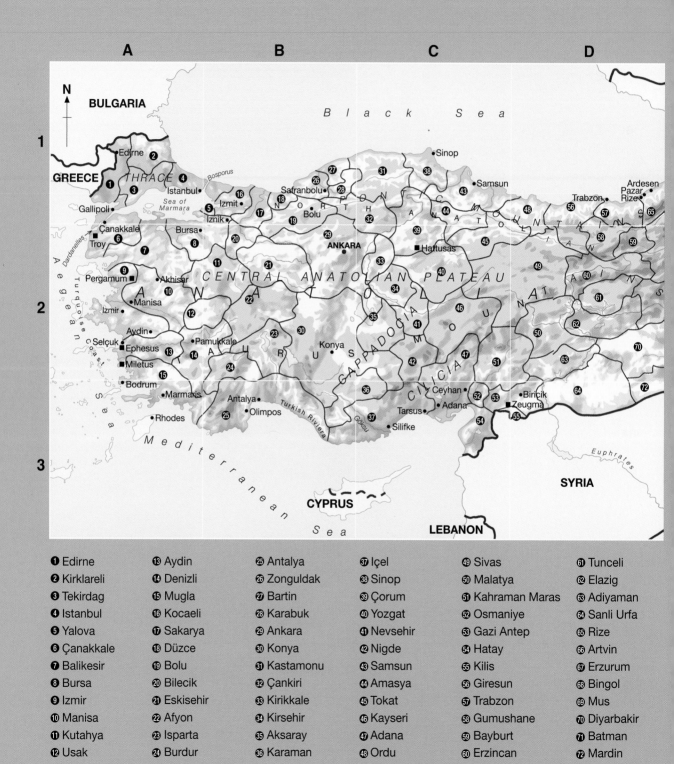

1. Edirne
2. Kirklareli
3. Tekirdag
4. Istanbul
5. Yalova
6. Çanakkale
7. Balikesir
8. Bursa
9. Izmir
10. Manisa
11. Kutahya
12. Usak
13. Aydin
14. Denizli
15. Mugla
16. Kocaeli
17. Sakarya
18. Düzce
19. Bolu
20. Bilecik
21. Eskisehir
22. Afyon
23. Isparta
24. Burdur
25. Antalya
26. Zonguldak
27. Bartin
28. Karabuk
29. Ankara
30. Konya
31. Kastamonu
32. Çankiri
33. Kirikkale
34. Kirsehir
35. Aksaray
36. Karaman
37. Içel
38. Sinop
39. Çorum
40. Yozgat
41. Nevsehir
42. Nigde
43. Samsun
44. Amasya
45. Tokat
46. Kayseri
47. Adana
48. Ordu
49. Sivas
50. Malatya
51. Kahraman Maras
52. Osmaniye
53. Gazi Antep
54. Hatay
55. Kilis
56. Giresun
57. Trabzon
58. Gumushane
59. Bayburt
60. Erzincan
61. Tunceli
62. Elazig
63. Adiyaman
64. Sanli Urfa
65. Rize
66. Artvin
67. Erzurum
68. Bingol
69. Mus
70. Diyarbakir
71. Batman
72. Mardin

E

RUSSIA

GEORGIA

T'BILISI

Hopa

66 · 73

Kars ·

ARMENIA

67 · 74 · 75

Mount Ararat ▲

76

· Malazgirt

IRAN

68 · 69

Mu rat

Lake Van

71 · 77 · 78

79

· Hasankeyf

80 · 81

· Mardin

IRAQ

● Capital city
● Major town
▲ Mountain peak
■ Ancient site

Feet		Meters
16,500		5,000
9,900		3,000
6,600		2,000
3,300		1,000
1,650		500
660		200
0		0

73 Ardahan
74 Kars
75 Igdir
76 Agri
77 Bitlis
78 Van
79 Siirt
80 Sirnak
81 Hakkari

Adana, C3
Aegean Sea, A2—A3
Anatolia, A2—E2
Ankara (Angora),
  C2
Antalya, B3
Ararat, Mount, E2
Ardesen, D1
Armenia, E1—E2
Aydin, A2
Azerbaijan, E2

Birecik, D2
Black Sea, A1—B1
Bodrum, A2
Bolu, B1
Bosporus Strait, B1
Bulgaria, A1
Bursa, B2

Çanakkale, A1
Cappadocia, C2
Central Anatolian
  Plateau, B2—D2
Ceyhan, C2
Cilicia, C2—C3
Cyprus, B3—C3

Dardanelles Strait,
  A1—A2

Edirne, A1
Ephesus, A2
Euphrates (river),
  D2—D3

Gallipoli, A1
Georgia, D1—E2
Göksu (river),
  B2—C3
Greece, A1—A3

Hasankeyf, E2
Hattusas, C2
Hopa, E1

Iran, E2
Iraq, E2—E3
Istanbul, B1
Izmir (Smyrna), A2
Izmit, B1
Iznik (Nicea), B1

Kars, E1
Konya (Iconium), B2

Lake Van, E2
Lebanon, C3

Malazgirt, E 2
Manisa, A2
Mardin, E2
Marmaris, A2
Mediterranean Sea,
  A2—C3
Miletus, A2
Murat (river), D2—
  E2

Olimpos, B3

Pamukkale, B2
Pazar, D1

Pergamum, A2
Pontic Mountains,
  B1—D1

Rhodes (Greece),
  A3
Rize, D1
Russia, D1—E1

Safranbolu, B1
Samsun, C1
Sea of Marmara,
  A1—B1
Silifke (Seleucia),
  C3
Sinop, C1
Syria, C3—E3

Tarsus, C3
T'bilisi, E1
Thrace, A1—B1
Tigris (river),
  D2—E3
Trabzon, D1
Troy, A2
Turkish Riviera, B3
Turquoise Coast,
  A1—A3

Zeugma, D3

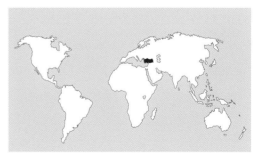

ECONOMIC TURKEY

Natural Resources

 Hydroelectricity

 Mining

Services

 Airport

 Port

 Tourism

Manufacturing

 Automobiles

 Chemicals

 Food Processing

 Textiles

 Tiles

Agriculture

 Cotton

 Hazelnuts

 Olives

 Tea

 Tobacco

ABOUT THE CULTURE

OVERVIEW

Turkey's mostly free-market economy is becoming increasingly driven by its industry and service sectors, although its traditional agriculture sector still accounts for about 25 percent of employment. Global economic conditions and a tighter fiscal policy had caused the Gross Domestic Product (GDP) to contract in 2009, but Turkey's well-regulated financial markets and banking system helped the country weather the global financial crisis. Still, growth dropped to about 2.6 percent in 2012. The slowdown is largely caused the continuing economic turmoil in Europe and uncertainty related to monetary policy-making, which has left the economy vulnerable to destabilizing shifts in investor confidence.

GROSS DOMESTIC PRODUCT (GDP)

$1.142 trillion (2012 estimate)

GDP PER CAPITA

$15,200 (2012 estimate)

GROWTH RATE

2.6 percent (2012 estimate)

CURRENCY

1 Turkish lira (TRY) = 100 kurush
Notes: 5, 10, 20, 50, 100 lira
Coins: Frequently used: 5 kurush, 10 kurush, 25 kurush, 50 kurush, 1 lira.
Rarely used: 1 kurush
USD 1 = TRY 1.99 (October 2013)

GDP SECTORS

Agriculture 9.1 percent, industry 27 percent, services 63.9 percent (2012 estimate)

WORKFORCE

27.3 million (2012 estimate)

UNEMPLOYMENT RATE

9.2 percent (2012 estimate)

POPULATION BELOW POVERTY LINE

16.9 percent (2010 estimate)

EXTERNAL DEBT

$336.9 billion (2012 estimate)

AGRICULTURAL PRODUCTS

Tobacco, citrus cotton, grain, olives, sugar beets, hazelnuts, pulses, livestock

INDUSTRIES

Automobiles, construction, food processing, electronics, lumber, mining, paper, petroleum, steel, textiles

NATURAL RESOURCES

Coal, iron ore, copper, chromium, antimony, mercury, gold, barite, borate, celestite (strontium), emery, feldspar, limestone, magnesite, marble, perlite, pumice, pyrites (sulfur), clay, arable land, hydropower

MAJOR EXPORTS

Apparel, foodstuffs, textiles, metal manufactures, transport equipment

MAJOR IMPORTS

Chemicals, fuels, machinery, semi-finished goods, transport equipment

CULTURAL TURKEY

Troy
Troy holds an enduring place in both literature and archeology because of the Trojan war. A replica of the infamous wooden horse stands among the ruins.

Istanbul
Previously known as Byzantium and later as Constantinople, Istanbul is the largest city in Turkey. The city is also on UNESCO's World Heritage List.

Iznik tiles
The town of Iznik, formerly known as Nicea, is famed for its blue tiles, made here since Byzantine times. The town remains a historical and cultural center today.

Cappadocia
The area is famous for its ancient churches that are hewn out of rock and decorated with wall paintings. Frescoes of early Christian icons can still be seen at protected sites in Cappadocia.

Hattusas
Hattusas is the site of the remains of the ancient capital of the Hittites. The Hittite empire dominated what is now central Turkey and northern Syria in 2 B.C.

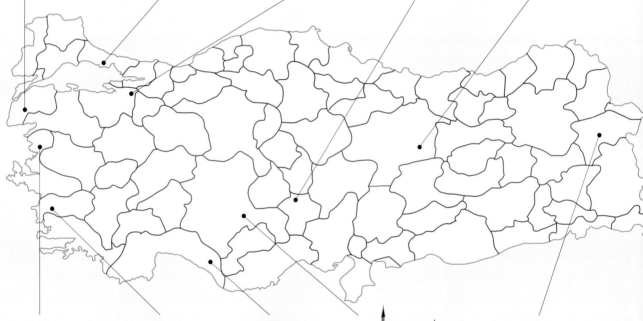

Pergamum
The ancient city of Pergamum, dating back to 4 B.C., was a center of Greek culture and learning. The city later became important to the Romans as an administrative center for Asia Minor. Ruins of temples and libraries indicate Pergamum's cultural and social importance.

Ephesus
In the ancient world, Ephesus was an important Greek city in Asia Minor. The Temple of Artemis at Ephesus was one of the seven wonders of the ancient world.

Aspendos
This is one of the best preserved theaters of the ancient world. It was built in 2 A.D. and designed by the famed Roman architect Zenon. The amphitheater, which can sit 15,000, is still in use today.

Mausoleum of Mevlan Jalal al-Din al-Rumi
Located in Konya, the museum houses the works of the founder of the Whirling Dervishes, Mevlana Jalal al-Din al-Rumi. The Whirling Dervishes perform in an annual festival in December.

Ishak Pasa Palace
Near the border with Iran, the town of Dogubeyazit is home to the 18th-century Ishak Pasa Palace, one of the last examples of Ottoman monumental architecture and one of the empire's most famous palaces. The palace was built on a hill and offers stunning views of nearby Mount Ararat, the legendary resting place of Noah's Ark.

ABOUT THE CULTURE

OFFICIAL NAME
Republic of Turkey

CAPITAL
Ankara

NATIONAL FLAG
Red with a vertical white crescent moon (the closed portion is toward the hoist side) and white five-pointed star centered just outside the crescent opening; the flag colors and designs closely resemble those on the banner of Ottoman Empire, which preceded modern-day Turkey; the crescent moon and star serve as insignia for the Turks, as well as being traditional symbols of Islam; according to legend, the flag represents the reflection of the moon and a star in a pool of blood of Turkish warriors. The flag was adopted only in 1936, but the crescent is believed to have been adopted as early as 340 BC. The star was added later in 1459 under the reign of Sultan Mehmet II.

POPULATION
80.7 million (2013 estimate)

AREA
251,827 square miles (652,230 square km)

PROVINCES
Adana, Adiyaman, Afyonkarahisar, Agri, Aksaray, Amasya, Ankara, Antalya, Ardahan, Artvin, Aydin, Balikesir, Bartin, Batman, Bayburt, Bilecik, Bingol, Bitlis, Bolu, Burdur, Bursa, Canakkale, Cankiri, Corum, Denizli, Diyarbakir, Duzce, Edirne, Elazig, Erzincan, Erzurum, Eskisehir, Gaziantep, Giresun, Gumushane, Hakkari, Hatay, Igdir, Isparta, Istanbul, Izmir (Smyrna), Kahramanmaras, Karabuk, Karaman, Kars, Kastamonu, Kayseri, Kilis, Kirikkale, Kirklareli, Kirsehir, Kocaeli, Konya, Kutahya, Malatya, Manisa, Mardin, Mersin, Mugla, Mus, Nevsehir, Nigde, Ordu, Osmaniye, Rize, Sakarya, Samsun, Sanliurfa, Siirt, Sinop, Sirnak, Sivas, Tekirdag, Tokat, Trabzon (Trebizond), Tunceli, Usak, Van, Yalova, Yozgat, Zonguldak

ETHNIC GROUPS
Turkish 70-75 percent, Kurdish 18 percent, other minorities 7-12 percent (2008 estimate)

OFFICIAL LANGUAGES
Turkish (official), Kurdish, other minority languages

MAJOR RELIGIONS
Muslim 99.8 percent (mostly Sunni), other 0.2 percent (mostly Christians and Jews)

LIFE EXPECTANCY
73.03 years; 71.09 years for men, 75.07 years for women (2013 estimate)

TIMELINE

IN TURKEY	IN THE WORLD

1900 B.C.
Beginning of Hittite civilization
1250 B.C.
War between Troy and Greece
660 B.C.
The Greeks founded the colony of Byzantium
A.D. 330
Emperor Constantine makes Byzantium the capital of the Eastern Roman empire and renames it Constantinople.
1000
The Turks arrive in Anatolia from East Asia.

1206–1368
Genghis Khan unifies the Mongols and starts conquest of the world. At its height, the Mongol Empire under Kublai Khan stretches from China to Persia and parts of Europe and Russia.

1243
The Mongols defeat Turkish Seljuk armies.
1288
Beginning of the Ottoman Empire after the fall of the Turkish Seljuk state
1453
Constantinople falls to the Ottomans
1520
The Ottoman Empire flourishes under Süleyman the Magnificent.
1683
The Ottoman army is defeated at Vienna, Austria.

1776
U.S. Declaration of Independence

1826
The Janissaries revolt and thousands of them are killed under the sultan's orders.

1914
World War I begins.

1918
Ottoman Empire defeated in World War I
1920–22
Period of the Turkish War of Independence
1923
Declaration of a Turkish Republic and the beginning of Atatürk's social and political reforms in the country.

1939
World War II begins.
1945
The United States drops atomic bombs on Hiroshima and Nagasaki. World War II ends.

1960
The army takes control of the Turkish state, and a period of military rule begins.
1974
Turkish troops invade Cyprus.
1990s
Kurds struggle for their rights in eastern and southeastern Turkey.
1993
Tansu Ciller becomes Turkey's first woman prime minister.

1997
Hong Kong is returned to China.

1999
Turkey is accepted as a candidate for membership in the European Union

IN TURKEY	IN THE WORLD
2001 The lira plummets as the economy tumbles.	**2001** Terrorists crash planes into New York, Washington D.C., and Pennsylvania.
2002 The AK party comes into power.	
2003 U.S. forces are not allowed to use Turkish air bases in the war with Iraq but use of Turkish airspace is allowed.	**2003** War in Iraq begins.
2004 Turkey signs protocol banning death penalty in all circumstances, a move welcomed in EU circles. Parliament approves penal reforms introducing tougher measures to prevent torture and violence against women.	**2004** Eleven Asia countries are hit by giant tsunami, killing at least 225,000 people.
2005 New lira currency introduced as six zeroes are stripped from old lira, ending an era in which banknotes were denominated in millions. Parliament approves amendments to new penal code after complaints that the previous version restricted media freedom.	**2005** Hurricane Katrina devastates the Gulf Coast of the United States.
2006 Parliament passes new anti-terror law which worries the EU and which rights groups criticize as an invitation to torture.	
2007 AK Party wins parliamentary elections. Abdullah Gul is elected president.	
2008 Parliament approves constitutional amendments which will pave the way for women to be allowed to wear the Islamic headscarf in universities.	
2009 PM Erdogan holds a rare meeting with the leader of the pro-Kurdish Democratic Society Party, Ahmet Turk, as part of efforts to solve the Kurdish problem politically.	**2009** Outbreak of flu virus H1N1 around the world
2010 Relations with Israel come under severe strain after nine Turkish activists are killed in a commando raid on an aid flotilla attempting to reach blockaded Gaza.	
2011 The ruling Justice and Development Party (AKP) wins resounding victory in general election. PM Erdogan embarks on third term in office.	**2011** Twin earthquake and tsunami disasters strike northeast Japan, leaving more than 14,000 dead and thousands more missing.
2013 Widespread protests and strikes erupt across the country with regards to the freedom of press and secularism.	

GLOSSARY

bakkal (BUCK-aal)
A small traditional grocery store

cevez (jeh-VEZ-eh)
A narrow-necked, long-handled pot used for making Turkish coffee

cirit (jer-IT)
A traditional Turkish sport in which competitors fight on horseback using javelins

darekh (duh-REH-keh)
A species of fish related to the herring

dolmus (doll-MUSH)
A communal bus that follows a set route but stops wherever required

gecekondu (GEDJ-erh KOHN-doo)
Squatter dwellings around the big cities

hammam (hah-MUM)
A Turkish bathhouse

harem (HAAR-em)
Quarters for the women and their children living in a sultan's palace

imam (ee-MUM)
A person of considerable spiritual authority; often the prayer leader at a mosque

kilim (KEE-lim)
A woven carpet with bold patterns

Koran (koo-RAN)
The Islamic holy book

lokanta (low-KUNT-a)
A Turkish restaurant

mevlud (mev-LOOD)
A prayer recited at a funeral

meyhane (may-HAH-nay)
A Turkish tavern

mihrab (meh-RUB)
A prayer niche showing the direction of Mecca

mimber (MIEM-behr)
The pulpit where the imam stands

muska (m-OO-ska)
A Turkish magical charm

namus (NAH-moose)
Honor, a highly regarded trait of Turkish males

nargile (nar-GEE-lay)
A Turkish hubble-bubble pipe

seranders (serh-AN-derhs)
Storehouses erected on stilts for storing corn

yayla (YAI-lah)
Rural houses built of stone to half their height and then completed in timber. The word also refers to summer cottages.

FOR FURTHER INFORMATION

BOOKS

Bainbridge, James. *Lonely Planet Turkey*. Oakland: Lonely Planet (Twelfth Edition), 2011.

Baring, Rose. *DK Eyewitness Travel Guide: Istanbul*. London: DK Travel, 2011.

Dubin, Marc, Yale, Pat, and Richardson, Terry. *Turkey* (Insight Guides). London: Apa Publications (Sixth Edition), 2011.

Finkel, Andrew. *Turkey: What Everyone Needs to Know*. New York: Oxford University Press, 2012.

Kinzer, Stephen. *Crescent and Star: Turkey Between Two Worlds*. New York: Farrar, Straus and Giroux (Revised edition), 2008.

Swan, Suzanne. *Turkey* (Eyewitness Travel Guides). London: DK Travel (Reprint edition), 2010.

Toynbee, Arnold Joseph. *Turkey: A Past and A Future*. Whitefish: Kessinger Publishing, 2010.

WEBSITES

Central Intelligence Agency World Factbook (select "Turkey" from the country list). www.cia.gov/cia/publications/factbook

Ministry of Culture and Tourism. www.kultur.gov.tr

Ministry of Foreign Affairs. www.mfa.gov.tr

Southeastern Anatolia Project. www.gap.gov.tr

Turkey's Official Tourism Portal. www.goturkey.com/

Turkish Embassy at Washington D.C. www.turkishembassy.org

U.S. Department of State Background Notes (select "Turkey" from the country list). www.state.gov/r/pa/ei/bgn

DVDS

Cities of the World Istanbul Turkey. TravelVideoStore.com, November 2009.

Rick Steves: Rick Steves' Greece and Turkey. Avalon Travel Publishing; May 2009.

MUSIC

Bhattacharya: Whirling Dervishes of Turkey & Syria (The Deben Bhattacharya Collection), DBC, 2011

The Henkesh Brothers, Yasmin Henkesh, and Artemis Mourat: Turkey/Egypt: Turkish Dance Favorites by the Henkesh Brothers, Sands of Time Music, June 2012

Various Artists—FM Records. *East Mediterranean Musical Instruments: "Oud" (Liban, Egypt, Turkey, Greece, Syria)*. FM Records, January 2011

BIBLIOGRAPHY

BOOKS

Bainbridge, James. *Lonely Planet Turkey.* Oakland: Lonely Planet (Twelfth Edition), 2011.

Baring, Rose. *DK Eyewitness Travel Guide: Istanbul.* London: DK Travel, 2011.

Dubin, Marc, Yale, Pat, and Richardson, Terry. *Turkey (Insight Guides).* London: Apa Publications (Sixth Edition), 2011.

Finkel, Andrew. *Turkey: What Everyone Needs to Know.* New York: Oxford University Press, 2012.

Kinzer, Stephen. *Crescent and Star: Turkey Between Two Worlds.* New York: Farrar, Straus and Giroux (Revised edition), 2008.

Swan, Suzanne. *Turkey (Eyewitness Travel Guides).* London: DK Travel (Reprint edition), 2010.

Toynbee, Arnold Joseph. *Turkey: A Past and A Future.* Whitefish: Kessinger Publishing, 2010.

WEBSITES

All About Turkey.com — National Parks of Turkey. www.allaboutturkey.com/millipark.htm

Digital Dialects — Turkish Language. www.digitaldialects.com/Turkish.htm

Enjoy Turkey.com. www.enjoyturkey.com

Lonely Planet — History of Turkey. www.lonelyplanet.com/turkey/history#227660

National Geographic Kids — Turkey. http://kids.nationalgeographic.com/kids/places/find/turkey/

Oil Warriors — Kirkpinar Wrestling Festival. www.pilotguides.com/destination_guide/middle-east-north-africa/turkey/kirkpinar_wrestling_festival.php

The Kurdish struggle for identity in Turkey. http://worldpress.org/Europe/3790.cfm

The Middle East Quarterly — Turkey's Military. www.meforum.org/2160/turkey-military-catalyst-for-reform

The People of Hemsin Hamshen. www.karalahana.com/english/archive/hemsin2.html

Turkey and European Union Relations. www.europeanunionplatform.org/

Turkish Cultural Foundation — The Traditional Game of Cirit. www.turkishculture.org/lifestyles/turkish-culture-portal/cirit/the-traditional-game-329.htm

Turkish Cultural Foundation — Turkish Cuisine. www.turkish-cuisine.org/english

Turkish Folk Dances. www.dunav.org.il/balkan_music_turkish.html#all

Turkish Odyssey.com — Turkish People. www.turkishodyssey.com/turkey/culture/people.htm

Uniquely Turkish Experience — The Turkish Bath Massage. www.passportchop.com/europe/turkey/turkish-bath-massage-hamam/

Whirling Dervishes (Mevlevi). www.turkeytravelplanner.com/go/CentralAnatolia/Konya/mevlevi.html

100 most useful words in Turkish. www.turkeytravelplanner.com/details/LanguageGuide/100words_lessons/

INDEX

INDEX